Born in _____, Co. Donegal, Fran____
in Dublin and lectures in English at S_____
Maynooth. He has also worked at the _____
Coleraine, and at University College, _____

For the Abbey Theatre he has writt__ _____
Baglady, and in 1985 the celebrated *Observe the Sons of Ulster
Marching Towards the Somme* which won many awards,
including the London *Evening Standard* Most Promising
Playwright Award, an Arts Council Bursary, the 1987 Ewart-
Biggs Peace Prize, the 1985 Harvey's Best Play Award and the
Cheltenham Literary Prize. His play *Innocence* (on the life of
Caravaggio) premièred at the Gate Theatre in October 1986. His
new version of Lorca's *Yerma* was produced at the Abbey
Theatre in May 1987 and a new version of Ibsen's *Rosmersholm*,
commissioned by the National Theatre of Great Britain, opened
in the same week. *Carthaginians* received its première during the
1988 Dublin Theatre Festival, and was also produced at the
Hampstead Theatre. His latest play, *Mary and Lizzie*, was
performed at the Barbican in 1989.

by the same author

HENRIK IBSEN'S
PEER GYNT

a new version by
FRANK McGUINNESS

from a literal translation by
Anne Bamborough

faber and faber
LONDON · BOSTON

For Barbara Fox

First published in 1990
by Faber and Faber Limited
3 Queen Square London WC1N 3AU

Photoset by Wilmaset, Birkenhead, Wirral
Printed in Great Britain by
Richard Clay Limited, Bungay, Suffolk

A CIP record for this book is available from
the British Library.

ISBN 0–571–14311–3

INTRODUCTION

A LONG NECK

As a student I specialized in Medieval Studies. To complement Old and Middle English I had to choose a second language. Old French, Old Irish, or Old Norse. I went with the Vikings. An excellent teacher, Rory McTurk, opened the sagas to me, the pleasures and perils of the poetry, Eddaic and Scaldic, their secret lair of kennings, the magnificent stories. My links with Northern Europe were forged.

In 1928 two men, one Irish, Micheál Mac Liammóir, and one English, Hilton Edwards, founded a theatre in Dublin, and called it the Gate. Their opening productions were Oscar Wilde's *Salome* and Ibsen's *Peer Gynt*. They had some neck. And they survived. The survivor who inherits their legacy at the Gate is Michael Colgan. He has also inherited their neck. To celebrate the theatre's sixtieth anniversary, he decided to mount both plays. I became part of this ambitious scheme in the following way. Stranded on a Sunday afternoon at Heathrow Airport for three hours, demented with boredom, I suddenly saw Colgan approaching me, smiling. This is dangerous. The following dialogue ensued.

MICHAEL: I was just thinking of you, McGuinness.
FRANK: You're looking for something, Colgan.
MICHAEL: *Peer Gynt*, in its entirety, for next year.
FRANK: Michael, you're mad.
MICHAEL: Frank, so are you.

Where do you start with *Peer Gynt*? Preferably with a Norwegian who knows and loves Ibsen the poet as much as Ibsen the playwright. By good fortune I had worked with Anne Bamborough from her literal version of *Rosmersholm* for the National Theatre of Great Britain, directed by Sarah Pia

Anderson. Anne's sensitivity to nuance, her accuracy of tone, the sheer generosity of her learning, these were my guide to Ibsen, and always ringing in my ears, her stricture, Ibsen is a poet, a great poet. I had freedom and chains, my favourite combination. It is also the only way to love Peer Gynt. And I admit it, I love him. Liar, blaggard, louse, drunk, violent, then shockingly, pitifully tender, mad as a tree, good, occasionally, to his mother, cracked about women, afraid of men, sorely needing his absent father, crazed with ambition, sick from failure, this creature I wouldn't let into my house, but I welcomed him charging into my head, for the pain, the terrible pain of Peer Gynt must be endured as well. It was endured through energy, that formidable energy of Ibsen, obsessing me, driving all before it, rampaging forward, taking the classic five-act form and inflating it beyond repair, planting dynamite beneath the unities of time and place, risking artistic suicide – that bleeding human pen at the end of Act Four – so that the theatre might never be the same again. The excitement of it can only be compared to discovering Shakespeare. Is it any wonder James Joyce at the age of eighteen knew who his master was and wrote his most sincere love letter to the dying Ibsen after the Irishman had read *When We Dead Awaken?* The Viking and the Celt up to glorious badness. *Peer Gynt* and *Ulysses* end by affirming love, having earned, miraculously, that right to affirmation. Here is the world and the mood is celebratory.

Ibsen is a northern writer. His is a Protestant mind, doubting itself profoundly. John Rosmer scrutinizes his motives with self-blinding clarity. Hedda Gabler burns Ejlert Lovborg's book as if it were a bible, cursing the babe of the new faith. Peer Gynt fails because he cannot stand alone. They betray their breed. In betrayal lies their destiny. Can they be forgiven? That's up to the audience. 'No coward's soul is mine,' declared Ibsen's spiritual ancestor, Emily Brontë, of stout Antrim clerical stock, and, like the best prophets, Ibsen lets his audience make its imaginative mind up for itself. At the core of the kenning there is no absolute meaning. Opaqueness is all. The sagas cool their narratives by deliberate refusal to elaborate. Things happen. Declare them. Here in the biggest sense of the description is a lonely imagination, tempered by pity, unflinching before terror, peeling an onion without crying.

More than this I can't, won't say about Ibsen. The result is in the writing. In *Rosmersholm* John Rosmer laments the loss of joy. From working on *Peer Gynt* I know now what a cry is there, for joy in its manifestations and perversions inform every episode of *Peer Gynt*. Rest assured, liberties have been taken. Rest even more assured, such liberties will be highlighted as evidence of ignorance or laziness. So be it, I'll argue for a sense of ironic parallels between Ibsen and Ireland's cultural dilemmas. My thanks again to Anne Bamborough – what omissions, inversions, errors and outrages are committed are mine. Thanks also to Shaun Davey, Mick Hughes and Joe Vanek for their work on the production. The director, Patrick Mason, gave the text life. Michael Colgan had the vision to produce it, getting the money from God knows where. I'm grateful for his long neck.

FRANK MCGUINNESS, February 1990

Peer Gynt was first performed at the Gate Theatre on 4 October 1988 as part of the Dublin Theatre Festival. For the purposes of the production the play was divided into three parts. The cast changed for each part, as follows:

Part One

PEER GYNT	Barry Lynch
REINDEER MAN	Tony Coleman
ÅSE	Doreen Hepburn
KARI	Kate Flynn
VILLAGE WOMAN	Hilary Fannin
MASTER OF CEREMONIES	Anthony Newfield
ASLAK	Jonathan Ryan
GROOM'S MOTHER	Liz Davis
GROOM'S FATHER	David Heap
MADS MOEN	Mark O'Regan
SOLVEIG'S FATHER	Scott Fredericks
SOLVEIG'S MOTHER	Joan Brosnan Walsh
SOLVEIG	Olwen Fouere
HELGA	Michèle Forbes
BRIDE'S FATHER	Alan Stanford
INGRID	Gabrielle Reidy
UPLAND GIRLS	Noelle Brown, Lynn Cahill, Hilary Fannin
GREEN WOMAN	Gabrielle Reidy
PIG	Tony Coleman
TWO-HEADED TROLL	Joan Brosnan Walsh, Liz Davis
OLD TROLL	Anthony Newfield
TROLL KING	Alan Stanford
HARPIES	Noelle Brown, Lynn Cahill, Hilary Fannin
BOY	Peter Holmes
BRAT	Jonathan Sharpe

WEDDING GUESTS/TROLLS/ BAILIFF'S MEN	Tony Coleman, Scott Fredericks, Duncan Hamilton, David Heap, Peter Holmes, Dermod Moore, Mark O'Regan, Jonathan Ryan, Jonathan Sharpe, Noelle Brown, Lynn Cahill, Hilary Fannin, Michèle Forbes

Part Two

PEER GYNT	Garrett Keogh
TRUMPETERSTRALE	David Heap
COTTON	Anthony Newfield
BALLON	Jonathan Ryan
VON EBERKOPF	Scott Fredericks
FIRST HORSEMAN	Dermod Moore
SECOND HORSEMAN	Jonathan Sharpe
THIRD HORSEMAN	Tony Coleman
OLD MONKEY	Michèle Forbes
MONKEYS	Noelle Brown, Lynn Cahill, Hilary Fannin
THIEF	Duncan Hamilton
RECEIVER	Peter Holmes
ANITRA	Olwen Fouere
BEGRIFFENFELDT	Alan Stanford
SHAFMANN	Tony Coleman
FIRST GUARD	Jonathan Sharpe
SECOND GUARD	Duncan Hamilton
THIRD GUARD	Peter Holmes
HUHU	Mark O'Regan
FELLAH	Dermod Moore
HUSSEIN	David Heap
BEDOUIN WOMEN/ ASYLUM INMATES	Noelle Brown, Joan Brosnan Walsh, Lynn Cahill, Liz Davis, Hilary Fannin, Michèle Forbes, Scott Fredericks, Anthony Newfield, Jonathan Ryan

ix

Part Three

PEER GYNT	Joe Dowling
CAPTAIN	Anthony Newfield
ABLE SEAMAN	Dermod Moore
LOOK-OUT	Peter Holmes
BOSUN	Tony Coleman
SHIP'S MATE	Duncan Hamilton
COOK	Jonathan Sharpe
STRANGE TRAVELLER	Gabrielle Reidy
PRIEST	Scott Fredericks
WIDOW	Joan Brosnan Walsh
MOURNER	Liz Davis
ASLAK	Jonathan Ryan
MADS MOEN	Mark O'Regan
AUCTIONEER	Anthony Newfield
VILLAGE MEN	Tony Coleman, Duncan Hamilton, Peter Holmes, Dermod Moore, Jonathan Sharpe
VILLAGE WOMEN	Joan Brosnan Walsh, Noelle Brown, Lynn Cahill, Liz Davis, Hilary Fannin
YOUTH	Barry Lynch
SHERIFF	Garrett Keogh
ÅSE	Doreen Hepburn
BUTTONMOULDER	Kate Flynn
TROLL KING	Alan Stanford
THIN MAN	David Heap
SHOOTING STAR	Michèle Forbes
SOLVEIG	Olwen Fouere
Director	Patrick Mason
Designer	Joe Vanek
Music	Shaun Davey
Lighting Designer	Mick Hughes

x

ACT ONE

SCENE I

*A hillside. A river flows. An old millhouse stands on the other side of
the river. It is a hot summer day.* PEER GYNT *comes down the
footpath. His mother,* ÅSE, *follows.*

ÅSE: Liar. You're a liar, Peer!

PEER GYNT: No!

ÅSE: Lying!

PEER GYNT: I'm not!

ÅSE: All right, swear, swear it's true!

PEER GYNT: Swear? Why?

ÅSE: You daren't. Dreams, all of it, pure dreams!

PEER GYNT: Truth, every word, every blessed word.

ÅSE: How do you have it in you to face your mother? The
harvest's ripe and you're in the mountains months on end,
our busiest time. Hunting. Reindeer. On the glacier. Then
it's home, not a stitch together, neither gun nor game.
Listen, I have my eyes open yet you still try to get me
believing stupid, bigman stories. So where was it you met
the buck?

PEER GYNT: West of here, round Gjeudin!

ÅSE: (*Laughs mockingly*) Of course, of course!

PEER GYNT: Feel the wind. Bit into me. Pushed me to him.
Behind the tree he was, nosing in the snow, snouting for
moss.

ÅSE: Of course, of course!

PEER GYNT: The breath stood in me. I listened. A scrape of the
hoof. See the shape of a horn. I move, gentle, belly on the
ground. Take a gander behind the slabs. The buck, fat,
shining, gorgeous, you've never set eyes on the like.

ÅSE: God protect us!

PEER GYNT: Bang! The bucko's on the ground, me on his back

the minute he's landed. Have him by the left ear. Knife
ready to drive itself into the skull. Mad roar out of him,
bastard standing on all fours, a back kick hits the weapon
out of my fist. He has me pinned about him, horns up my
leg have me fucked like I'm finished, then he's off –

ÅSE: Sweet Jesus!

PEER GYNT: Hammers of hell along the ridge –

ÅSE: Sweet Jesus!

PEER GYNT: You know the ridge on the Gjeudin mountain?
Three miles long, sharp as scythe. The water's like falling
when you're sleeping in the dark, miles beneath you. I've
never seen such a hero as this bucko. We were like eagles
striking the sun. Nothing between us – I'm growing dizzy,
just the water and the air all swimming like feathers. I
could feel the ice bursting. I could see the shore. I could
hear nothing. The wind was a ghost and we were dancing,
singing, all in a ring. Sights and sounds.

ÅSE: Lord, watch over me.

PEER GYNT: Next thing, here's the edge, a bird starts in the
rock cawing, wings beating, mad in the rock, hiding next
to the bucko's foot. He turns half round, leap in the air,
two of us cast into the deep.
(ÅSE *staggers and grabs a tree trunk.*)
Down we fall, down and down, and something's shining
like a beast's belly. Ma, see the water, it's reflecting us,
falling and rising with the same wild speed.
(ÅSE *gasps for air.*)

ÅSE: Peer, God love us, tell me quick.

PEER GYNT: The sky and the water touched us together. Horns
crashing and the water had rabies. We lay spent and
flowing. Somehow or other, we reached the shore to the
north, Ma. The buck swam, me hanging on to him. Then I
came home.

ÅSE: Where's the buck, Peer?

PEER GYNT: Lying there likely. (*He snaps his fingers and turns his heel.*) If you find him he's yours.

ÅSE: You could have broken your neck, your legs, your spine. Holy God, thank you for saving my son. Your trousers are torn – let them go, when I think what you were spared – (*She stops suddenly, her mouth and eyes widen. For a time she is silent. Then she bursts out*) The devil put that into your mouth. Christ above, the lies, the lies. I know that yarn from years ago. It happened to Gudbrank Glesne, not you.

PEER GYNT: Things can happen twice.

ÅSE: Lies can wear new clothes and let on they're gentlemen. Liars, birds of a feather, lying to a body and leaving her stupid with fear. Lie that well she doesn't know words she's listened to since she was a lassie.

PEER GYNT: If that weren't from your mouth, it would be broken.

ÅSE: God grant me peace in the grave. Peer, you're lost, you will be lost.

PEER GYNT: Poor Ma, dear Ma, were you ever wrong? Give us a smile, be happy.

ÅSE: Me, happy? When I've a pig for a son? I'm a widow woman, and you break me to the bone. (*She weeps.*) What are we as a family? Something once, in the days of your father's father. He had money, but your father gave it legs to walk on. Wasted it. Bought land and went begging company. Come Christmas, glass and bottle smashed on the wall behind him.

PEER GYNT: (*Sings*) 'Have you gone like the snows of last winter?'

ÅSE: Respect your mother. Look at the farm. Every second window stuffed with rags. Neither hedge nor fence up. Cattle at the mercy of wind and rain. Fields lying barren. I'm the one who pays the month's due.

PEER GYNT: Old woman's talk. Stop. We're down, then we're up again, that's luck.

ÅSE: Luck? What luck we have is salt spilt. But Christ, aren't you the great man? Full of pride. Smart, like the time the Copenhagen priest asked your name. Peer Gynt. He swore it was fit for a prince. Your father gave him horse and sleigh. Thanks for the friendly words. Everything rosy in the garden. Could you move about here without falling over ones stuffing their bellies with grub and drink? Where are they when you're wanting? The day money marches out with its bag on its back, the house empties. (*She dries her eyes with her apron.*) A strapping man, look at you. Should you not look to your ailing mother. She's old. Should you not watch the farm? Defend what's yours by right. (*She weeps.*) Lord, what good is it? Much good out of you, waster. In the house you're sitting by the fire picking out coals. Outside no girl comes near you. You shame me in every quarter. The worst thugs in the parish you fight.

PEER GYNT: Give me peace.

ÅSE: Deny you were the ringleader in the fistfight at Lunde. Like a pack of dogs. You broke a man's arm.

PEER GYNT: Who gave you this gossip?

ÅSE: The women heard the roaring.

PEER GYNT: Aye, it was me roaring.

ÅSE: You?

PEER GYNT: Yes, Mother, I got the hiding.

ÅSE: What are you saying?

PEER GYNT: Strong man, quick on his feet.

ÅSE: Who?

PEER GYNT: Aslak, the blacksmith, as you said.

ÅSE: Jesus, I could spit. That cissy windbag, that pile of drunken guts, he beat you up? (*She weeps again.*) I've had some shame piled up on me, but was there ever worse? Are you such a drink of water?

PEER GYNT: Whether I'm battered or I batter, will you crucify me? (*He laughs.*) Go easy, Mother.

ÅSE: Is this another lie?

4

PEER GYNT: Yes, dry your eyes. (*He knots his left fist.*) This
boyo nailed the blacksmith down. The other was my
hammer –

ÅSE: Will you be the death of me?

PEER GYNT: You deserve better, twenty thousand times better.
Trust me, Mother, you'll be honoured above all else here.
Just wait until I do something really great.

ÅSE: You?

PEER GYNT: Luck brings what it likes.

ÅSE: Bring you to your senses. Bring you to the tear in your
trousers.

PEER GYNT: I will be king. I will be emperor.

ÅSE: God help me, there goes what's left of his reason.

PEER GYNT: But I will. Give me time.

ÅSE: Give him time, yes. Name fit for a prince. Do I remember
right?

PEER GYNT: Wait and see, Mother.

ÅSE: Hold your tongue. Cracked, every part of you. You spent
your time lying when you might have won the Hagstead
girl. If you wanted to, you could have bagged that one with
no bother.

PEER GYNT: Do you think so?

ÅSE: She rules the roost over her father. He might have his ways
but Ingrid gets her way. Where she goes, the old drunk
hobbles after her. (*She starts to weep again.*) Peer, she has
money. Land. Think, Peer. Had you wanted, you could
have been the lucky man, you, running around in rags.

PEER GYNT: Come on, we'll go and win her.

ÅSE: Where?

PEER GYNT: Hagstead.

ÅSE: Young fella, that door's closed.

PEER GYNT: How?

ÅSE: It breaks my heart. The chance lost. Luck was given and
taken.

PEER GYNT: Oh?

5

ÅSE: You were riding reindeer, falling through the air. Mads
    Moen fell on that girl.
PEER GYNT: What? That heap of sticks? Him?
ÅSE: She's taking him as hers.
PEER GYNT: Wait. I'll get the horse and cart.
ÅSE: Spare yourself. Useless bother. The wedding's tomorrow.
PEER GYNT: Then I'll be there tonight.
ÅSE: That's right, risk the world's mockery.
PEER GYNT: Ma, forget about the cart. The mare needs time to
    saddle.
    (*He lifts* ÅSE *up.*)
ÅSE: Let go of me.
PEER GYNT: I'll carry you to the wedding breakfast. (*He wades
    into the river.*)
ÅSE: Lord have mercy – Peer, we're drowning.
PEER GYNT: I was born to meet a gentler death.
ÅSE: They'll hang you.
    (PEER *pulls her hair.*)
PEER GYNT: Skip and jump, Peer and the buck –
ÅSE: Are you man or maniac?
PEER GYNT: I'll be the buck, and you be Peer –
ÅSE: Donkey.
PEER GYNT: Wag your tongue. Harm nobody. Play with me –
ÅSE: Don't let go.
PEER GYNT: We've reached the whirling part.
ÅSE: I'm not worth a penny.
    (PEER *wades ashore.*)
PEER GYNT: Give the buck a nice big kiss. Say thank you for
    the ride.
    (ÅSE *bites his ear.*)
ÅSE: Thank you for the ride.
PEER GYNT: That was mean.
ÅSE: Let go of me.
PEER GYNT: The wedding breakfast. You speak up for me. You

6

know what's what. Talk to the old boy. Say Mads Moen is
nothing –

ÅSE: Let go.

PEER GYNT: Then say Peer Gynt is a man, a splendid man.

ÅSE: Be sure of it. I'll sing your praises up and down. I'll tell
them all your dirty devil's tricks – loud and clear, I'll tell –

PEER GYNT: Will you?

(ÅSE *kicks in rage*.)

ÅSE: I won't stop telling the old man until he sets the dogs on
you like a tinker –

PEER GYNT: Then I'll go alone.

ÅSE: You do, but I'll be following.

PEER GYNT: Mother dear, you're not strong enough –

ÅSE: Am I not? I could crush stone, I'm strong enough. Eat
flint, if you like. Let go of me.

PEER GYNT: If you promise –

ÅSE: Nothing. I'll be there with you. They'll know who you are.

PEER GYNT: You'll stay here.

ÅSE: Never.

PEER GYNT: I won't let you.

ÅSE: What will you do?

PEER GYNT: See the millhouse? See the roof? See you, you're on
it. (*He lifts her up*.)

ÅSE: (*Shouts*) Lift me down.

PEER GYNT: But will you listen?

ÅSE: Balderdash.

PEER GYNT: Dear Mother, I intercede –

(ÅSE *throws a turf at him*.)

ÅSE: This minute, down, Peer, lift me.

PEER GYNT: I would if I could, but I can't, so I shan't.

ÅSE: Donkey.

PEER GYNT: Don't kick.

ÅSE: If I could fart you from this world –

PEER GYNT: Mother, shame on you –

(ÅSE *spits*.)

Give me your blessing for this journey. Will you?

ÅSE: I will give you a hiding, big and all as you are.

PEER GYNT: Goodbye, Mother dear. Have patience. I won't be
    long. (PEER *goes, turns around, lifts a finger warningly*.) Try
    to remember, don't kick. (*He goes.*)

ÅSE: Peer. God help me, he's going. Killer, liar, you, listen. No,
    he's across the field. (*She shouts.*) Help me, I'm fainting.
    (*Two women with bags on their backs come down to the
    millhouse.*)

KARI: Christ, who's shouting?

ÅSE: Me.

KARI: Åse? Look at that one – rising above herself.

ÅSE: Jesus send I was riding to heaven.

KARI: God go with you.

ÅSE: Get me a ladder. I want to get down. Peer, God damn
    you –

KARI: Your son?

ÅSE: You said it. Did you see how he treats me?

KARI: I'll speak out for you.

ÅSE: Just help me. I have to head straight for Hagstead.

KARI: Is he there? He'll get what's coming to him. The
    blacksmith is coming to the breakfast.
    (ÅSE *wrings her hands.*)

ÅSE: Jesus, my son, they'll take his life. They'll eat him without
    salt this day.

KARI: So they say. That's his luck. Ah well, God's good. The
    way of the world. Egvind Anders, come here to us.

MAN'S VOICE: What's wrong?

KARI: Peer Gynt's perched his mother up on the roof.

SCENE 2

*A small hill, bushes and heather. The country road is behind, a
fence between. Coming along the footpath,* PEER GYNT *walks
quietly to the fence, stops, looks out to the open view.*

8

PEER GYNT: Hagstead. Soon make it. (*He steps halfway across the fence, hesitates*) Ingrid, are you lonely sitting at home? (*He shades his eyes and looks across.*) No, the place is black with wedding people. Like midges. (*He draws back his leg.*) I can hear the sneers behind my back. Ears burning with whispers. (*He walks away from the fence.*)
(*Absentmindedly, he pulls at some leaves.*) If I'd a drop of the hard stuff, slip in without being noticed, if nobody knew me – something worth drinking – then to hell with them laughing. (*He looks around as if frightened, then hides.*)
(*People with baskets of food walk past to the wedding breakfast.*)

FATHER: The father liked the bottle and the mother's not well.

WOMAN: Is it a wonder the boy's an eejit?
(*They walk on.*)

PEER GYNT: (*Appears and looks after them. He speaks quietly*) Was that me they were talking about? (*He gives a forced shrug.*) Let them talk. Slander won't kill me. (*He throws himself on the ground, lying for a long time, his hands under his head, staring up into the air.*) Look at that cloud. Strange. Like a horse with a man on it. Saddled and harnessed. An old woman rides on a broom behind it. (*He laughs a little to himself.*) It's Ma. Scowling and shouting. You brute beast you, Peer. (*Little by little he closes his eyes.*) Yes, now the wind's up her. Peer Gynt's at the head of a mighty troop. Silver plumes and four gold shoes on the horse. He's wearing gloves and a sword and scabbard. The coat's long and lined with silk. His splendid train follows, but none compares with the proud glitter of him in the saddle. He's in the sun and the people beneath him lift their hats in homage. The women all know Peer Gynt the Emperor and his thousand men. He flings out gold like gravel. All hands in this parish will be rich as lords. Peer Gynt sails the ocean up in the sky. The Emperor of England raises his crown and says –

(*A crowd passes by the other side of the fence.* ASLAK *the smith among them.*)

ASLAK: Look at Peer Gynt, the drunken pig.

(PEER *stands halfway up.*)

PEER GYNT: What do you say, Emperor?

ASLAK: (*Leans on the fence, smirking*) Get up, boy.

PEER GYNT: What in the hell do you want?

ASLAK: The boozing at Lunde is still affecting him.

PEER GYNT: (*Leaps up*) Move while you still can.

ASLAK: I will, but where did you spring from? You were six weeks away –

PEER GYNT: I've done strange work.

ASLAK: (*Winks at the others*) Tell us all, Peer.

(*Silence.*)

ASLAK: Are you going to Hagstead?

PEER GYNT: No.

ASLAK: Once upon a time your woman there had her eye on you, so they say.

PEER GYNT: You black crow.

ASLAK: (*Draws back a little*) Don't worry yourself, Peer. If Ingrid doesn't want you, others will. Aren't you John Gynt's son? Head for the farm, young and old ones waiting. Sheep for the slaughter.

PEER GYNT: Go to hell.

ASLAK: There's one who must want you. Good luck. I'll give the bride your best wishes.

(*They leave laughing, and whispering.*)

PEER GYNT: (*Stamps his feet*) Jesus, had I a butcher's knife to cut the laughing from their throats . . . (*He looks around suddenly.*) Who's there? Who's sniggering? I was sure – no, nobody. Home, to my mother – (*He moves and stops, listening to the wedding party. He rubs his leg.*) Good Christ, the very floor is dancing. Like the sound of water leaping. Look at the shower of women. God damn me, I'll go in among them. (*He leaps over the fence and goes down the road.*)

SCENE 3

The front of the farm buildings at Hagstead. The main house is set furthest back. It is full of guests. The fiddler sits on the table. The MASTER OF CEREMONIES *stands by the door. The cook goes back and forth between the buildings. Other people engage in conversation. A* WOMAN *joins a group sitting on some tree trunks.*

WOMAN: The bride? She shed a tear, but sure who'd notice?

MASTER OF CEREMONIES: Slack your thirsts, boys and girls.

MAN: Thanks very much, but it's flowing mighty.

    (*A* YOUTH *runs by with a* GIRL, *calling to the fiddler.*)

YOUTH: Let it rip, boy, let it rip.

GIRL: We want to see the grass dancing.

    (GIRLS *dance in a ring about a* BOY.)

GIRL ONE: What do you make of him?

GIRL TWO: We've landed a fair one.

GIRL THREE: Come on, boy, how's your leg?

BOY: Do you want to come under and have a feel?

    (*Whimpering, the bridegroom approaches his* FATHER. *He is talking to a group of others. The* GROOM *pulls his father's jacket.*)

GROOM: Da, she doesn't want to. She's very proud.

FATHER: What doesn't she want to?

GROOM: She's locked herself in.

FATHER: Then go and find the key.

GROOM: I don't know how.

FATHER: Amadán eejit.

    (*The* GROOM *wanders across the court. A* YOUTH *calls from behind the house.*)

YOUTH: Ladies, prepare yourselves for action. Peer Gynt is come amongst us.

ASLAK: (*Just arrived*) Who invited him?

MASTER OF CEREMONIES: Nobody.

ASLAK: If he speaks, don't listen.

(*A* GIRL *addresses the others.*)

GIRL: No, we'll pretend we've never set eyes on him.

(PEER *enters, full of life and excited. He stops in front of the group, clapping his hands.*)

PEER GYNT: Who's the girl with the lightest foot?

GIRL ONE: I'm not.

GIRL TWO: Nor me.

GIRL THREE: Nor me neither.

PEER GYNT: You then, before a better one –

GIRL FOUR: Don't bother me.

PEER GYNT: So it's you –

GIRL FIVE: I'm going home.

PEER GYNT: Are you mad? In the night that's in it?

(*After a silence* ASLAK *speaks under his breath.*)

ASLAK: She's dancing with an old man over there.

PEER GYNT: Where are the ones to dance with?

MAN: Go and find them.

(PEER *suddenly grows quiet. Surreptitiously and shyly, he glances towards the crowd. They look at him, not speaking. Whichever group he approaches is silent. When he goes away, they stare after him, smiling.* PEER *speaks quietly to himself.*)

PEER GYNT: Looks that could kill and minds that would cut you. (*He slinks along the fence.*)

(SOLVEIG, *with little* HELGA *by the hand, comes into the yard along with her parents.*

A man speaks to PEER GYNT.)

MAN: Strangers. From the west.

SECOND MAN: From Hedalen. That's right.

(*As they enter,* PEER *steps in front of them. Pointing at* SOLVEIG, *he asks her father*)

PEER GYNT: May I dance with your daughter?

SOLVEIG'S FATHER: You may, but we must first go in and pay
   our respects. (*They go in.*)
   (*The* MASTER OF CEREMONIES *offers* PEER *a drink.*)
MASTER OF CEREMONIES: Since you're here, you'll have a
   drink.
PEER GYNT: Thanks, I'm here to dance, no thirst in me.
   (*The* MASTER OF CEREMONIES *goes away.* PEER *looks to the
   house and laughs.*)
   Did you ever see the like? Beautiful. Eyes glued to her
   shoes and the white apron. Clinging to her mother's skirts
   and her prayerbook in a cloth. I must look at that girl.
YOUTH: (*Comes out with others*) What, Peer, are you leaving the
   dance?
PEER GYNT: No.
YOUTH: Then you're heading the wrong way.
PEER GYNT: Let me through.
YOUTH: Are you afraid of the blacksmith?
PEER GYNT: Me, afraid?
YOUTH: Do you not remember the other evening at Lunde?
SOLVEIG: (*Appears in the doorway*) Isn't it you who's the boy
   who wanted to dance?
PEER GYNT: Me indeed. Can't you tell?
   (*He takes her hand.*)
   Come on.
SOLVEIG: Mother said not too far.
PEER GYNT: Mother said? Mother said! Were you born last
   year?
SOLVEIG: You're mocking me.
PEER GYNT: You're like a child. Are you grown up?
SOLVEIG: I was confirmed last spring.
PEER GYNT: Tell me your name, girl. It makes talking easier.
SOLVEIG: Solveig. What's yours?
PEER GYNT: Peer Gynt.
SOLVEIG: (*Pulls back her hand*) Oh God.
PEER GYNT: What's wrong?

SOLVEIG: My stocking's loose. I have to tie it. (*She draws away from him.*)

(*The* GROOM *pulls at his mother.*)

GROOM: Ma, she won't –

GROOM'S MOTHER: Won't what?

GROOM: She won't, Ma.

GROOM'S MOTHER: What?

GROOM: Open the door.

GROOM'S FATHER: You should be locked in the byre.

GROOM'S MOTHER: Let him be, poor lamb, he'll be grand.

(*They walk away. A youth comes with a whole swarm from dancing.*)

YOUTH: Drop of brandy, Peer?

PEER GYNT: No.

YOUTH: Just a sip.

PEER GYNT: (*Looks at him darkly*) Have you got any?

YOUTH: Could have. (*He takes out a flask and drinks.*)

YOUTH: Hair on your chest. Well?

PEER GYNT: Let me sample. (*He drinks.*)

YOUTH TWO: Sample mine as well.

PEER GYNT: No.

YOUTH TWO: Come on, don't be a fool. Drink up, Peer.

PEER GYNT: All right, give us a drop. (*He drinks.*)

GIRL: Come on, we'll move.

PEER GYNT: Afraid of me, girl?

YOUTH THREE: Who isn't?

YOUTH FOUR: You showed you knew your stuff at Lunde.

PEER GYNT: I might know even more if I'm roused.

CROWD: Tell us, tell us, what more could you do?

PEER GYNT: Tomorrow.

CROWD: Tonight.

GIRL: Can you cast spells, Peer?

PEER GYNT: I can raise the devil.

MAN: So could my granny.

PEER GYNT: Liar. I once charmed him into a nut through a
    little wormhole.
CROWD: Get away.
PEER GYNT: He swore, he wept, he promised me this and that –
YOUTH: He was stuck in there?
PEER GYNT: I plugged the hole with a peg. You should have
    heard him buzzing.
GIRL: Imagine that.
PEER GYNT: Just like a bumble bee.
GIRL: Is he still stuck inside the nut?
PEER GYNT: No, the devil's loose. Because of him the
    blacksmith turned against me.
YOUTH: How come?
PEER GYNT: I went to the forge to see if he'd crack the skull
    from the nut. He promised and put it on the anvil. But
    Aslak is a messer. He grabbed the sledgehammer –
YOUTH: Did he beat the devil to death?
PEER GYNT: He struck like a man, but the devil's the devil. He
    shot like a flame through the roof. Split the wall asunder.
YOUTH: And the blacksmith?
PEER GYNT: Aslak? Stood there with his hands half-burned off.
    Never broke breath to me since. (*Laughter*.)
MAN: Good yarn, good yarn.
YOUTH: Nearly his best.
PEER GYNT: Do you think I'm making it up?
MAN: No, you're innocent of that charge. I learned most of it
    from my grandfather.
PEER GYNT: That's a lie. It happened to me.
MAN: So does everything.
PEER GYNT: (*Shrugs*) Listen, I can charge through the sky. I
    can do plenty, if you'd like to know.
    (*Laughter*.)
YOUTH: Go on, Peer, charge through the sky.
CROWD: Go on, Peer, go on.

PEER GYNT: Don't bother begging me, I'll blast you apart. The whole parish will fall at my feet.

OLD MAN: Off with his head.

MAN: Donkey.

YOUTH: Big mouth.

MAN: Liar.

PEER GYNT: You wait, you'll see.

DRUNK: You wait, you'll have your coat dusted.

MAN: Your back beat blue, your eye painted black.

(*The crowd disperses. The older ones are angry, the younger ones laugh mockingly.*

The GROOM *moves towards* PEER GYNT.)

GROOM: Is it true you can ride through the air, Peer?

PEER GYNT: The only man, Mods, I'm telling you.

GROOM: They say there's a cloak makes a body vanish. Have you that too?

PEER GYNT: It's a hat, you mean. Yes. I've got it. (*He turns away.*)

(*Leading* HELGA *by the hand,* SOLVEIG *walks across the yard. Brightening up,* PEER *goes towards them.*)

Solveig. Nice of you to come. (*He takes hold of her wrist.*) I'll lift you off your feet as if you're flying.

SOLVEIG: Let me go.

PEER GYNT: Why?

SOLVEIG: You are so wild.

PEER GYNT: So's the buck when the summer's dawning. Come on, girl. Don't be awkward.

(SOLVEIG *withdraws her arm.*)

SOLVEIG: I daren't.

PEER GYNT: Why?

SOLVEIG: You've been drinking. (*She walks away with* HELGA.)

PEER GYNT: Would I'd a knife sticking through them – each and every one of them.

(*The* GROOM *prods* PEER *with his elbow.*)

GROOM: Could you help me get in to the bride?

PEER GYNT: Bride? Where?

GROOM: The storehouse.

PEER GYNT: Oh.

GROOM: Have a go, Peer Gynt, come on.

PEER GYNT: No, do it without me. (*A thought hits him. He says slowly and pointedly*) Ingrid, in the storehouse? (*He draws nearer to* SOLVEIG.) Have you thought about it?
(SOLVEIG *tries to leave.* PEER GYNT *blocks her way.*)
Does it shame you I look like a beggar?

SOLVEIG: It doesn't, and you don't.

PEER GYNT: So I've a drop taken. That was out of spite. You offended me. Come on then.

SOLVEIG: Daren't now, even if I wanted to.

PEER GYNT: What scares you?

SOLVEIG: Father.

PEER GYNT: Father? One of the quiet ones, is he? Holy, drooping head. Answer me.

SOLVEIG: Answer what?

PEER GYNT: Your father's a breastbeater? You too, and your mother? Answer me now.

SOLVEIG: Give my head peace.

PEER GYNT: No. (*He lowers his voice urgently and frighteningly.*) I can turn into a troll. Come twelve tonight, I'll come to your bed, hissing and spitting. Do you think it's a cat? It's me, draining your blood into a cup. Your little sister, I'll devour her. Do you know at night I'm a werewolf, biting your bones through to your back. (*He changes his tone and begs as if afraid.*) Dance with me, Solveig.

SOLVEIG: (*Looks at him darkly*) You have been cruel. (*She goes into the house.*)
(*The* GROOM *comes wandering in again.*)

GROOM: If you give us a hand, I'll see you have a bull.

PEER GYNT: Come on.
(*They go behind the house. A large crowd come up from the dancing place. Most are drunk. There is noise and uproar.*

Together with some older people, SOLVEIG, HELGA *and their parents come out the door.* ASLAK *the smith is in the front of the crowd.*)

ASLAK: Hold your peace. (*He takes off his jacket.*) Day of judgement. Settle it here. Whether Peer Gynt or I will hit the ground.

VOICE: Let them fight.

MAN: Only a squabble.

ASLAK: To hell with words, it's fists we need.

SOLVEIG'S FATHER: Control yourself, man.

HELGA: Will they hit him, Mother?

YOUTH: Better just to laugh at his lies.

MAN: Kick him out of the company.

ANOTHER MAN: Spit in his face.

(ASLAK *throws down his jacket.*)

ASLAK: I'll strangle the useless bugger.

(SOLVEIG'S MOTHER *speaks to* SOLVEIG.)

SOLVEIG'S MOTHER: Do you see how they look on that halfwit?

(ÅSE *enters with a stick in her hand.*)

ÅSE: Is my son here? He'll feel my hard wallop. He'll feel it.

(ASLAK *spits in his hands and nods to* ÅSE.)

ASLAK: Hang him.

ÅSE: What? Hang my Peer? Try if you dare. This is Åse and I have teeth and I have claws. Where is he? Peer?

(*The* GROOM *enters running to his parents.*)

GROOM: Daddy, Mammy.

GROOM'S FATHER: What's wrong?

GROOM: Imagine, Peer Gynt –

ÅSE: Have they killed him?

GROOM: No. Peer Gynt – up on the hill, look.

CROWD: He's got the bride.

(ÅSE *lowers the stick.*)

ÅSE: The brute beast.

ASLAK: (*Thunderstruck*) At the mountain's edge. He's limbing it like a goat.

(*The* GROOM *is crying.*)

GROOM: Ma, he carries her like you'd carry a pig.

(ÅSE *threatens up to* PEER.)

ÅSE: Would that you landed down here – (*She cries out in fear*)
Watch your step well where it's steep.

(INGRID'S FATHER, *a farmer, enters without a hat, white with
rage.*)

INGRID'S FATHER: I will wring his scraggy neck for thieving the
bride.

ÅSE: God strike me dead if I let you.

ACT TWO

SCENE I

High up on a mountain path. PEER GYNT *walks along, hurriedly and sullenly. Half-dressed in bridal finery,* INGRID *tries to pull him back.*

PEER GYNT: Get away from me.

INGRID: (*Weeps*) After this, where?

PEER GYNT: As far away as you like. What's it to me?

INGRID: (*Wrings her hands*) Desertion.

PEER GYNT: Useless fighting. We all go our own way.

INGRID: We sinned – we sinned twice. That unites us.

PEER GYNT: Devil take the memory. Devil take all women. All but one –

INGRID: Which one?

PEER GYNT: Not you.

INGRID: Who then?

PEER GYNT: Get back to your house. Get back to your da.

INGRID: Oh God, love –

PEER GYNT: Shut it.

INGRID: You can't mean what you're saying.

PEER GYNT: I can, I do.

INGRID: First I'm taken, then I'm thrown –

PEER GYNT: What do you have to offer?

INGRID: Hagstead farm. More besides.

PEER GYNT: Where's your prayerbook wrapped in cloth? Where's your red mane down your neck? Do you gaze gently at your apron? Do you cling to your mother's skirts? Answer.

INGRID: No, but –

PEER GYNT: Were you confirmed last spring then?

INGRID: No, but, Peer –

20

PEER GYNT: Where's the modest look about you? If I beg, would you refuse?

INGRID: Christ, I think he's lost his senses.

PEER GYNT: Is it the Sabbath when I see you? Answer.

INGRID: No, but –

PEER GYNT: Then what are you?

INGRID: You led me astray. (*She weeps.*)

PEER GYNT: You offered.

INGRID: I was desperate.

PEER GYNT: I was drunk.

INGRID: (*Threatens*) Yes, and you'll pay a high price.

PEER GYNT: Let it cost me what you like, it will still be cheap.

INGRID: Are you set on this?

PEER GYNT: Like rock.

INGRID: Right then, watch who wins. (*She walks downward.*)
    (PEER *stands quietly, then calls out.*)

PEER GYNT: Devil take the memory, devil take all women.
    (INGRID *turns and calls up mockingly.*)

INGRID: All but one.

PEER GYNT: Yes, all but one.
    (*They exit separately.*)

SCENE 2

A storm is brewing. A mountain barn, with swampland. In despair ÅSE *is calling, looking in all directions.* SOLVEIG *has difficulty keeping up with her. Her parents and* HELGA *are a little behind them.* ÅSE *tears her hair, gesticulating.*

ÅSE: The earth's raised its ire against me, sky and water and stone. Jesus throws fogs against him, he'll lose his way. The water's crafty, it will take him. The stone will fall and strike him dead. And the people out to kill him. Damned if they try, I won't lose him. Is he a son of mine at all? It's the devil tempting him. (*She turns to* SOLVEIG.) Can I credit this? Him the liar, him, the sweet mouth, him that never did a good day's work in his life – I could either laugh or cry. In want and wailing we stuck together. You should know, my husband drank. I sat with the child at home. Me and Peer. Yes, we told our stories. Kings and trolls, all kinds of beasts. Brides were taken, that as well. Who would have thought those damned stories stuck inside him – (*She is frightened again.*) Jesus, a scream? Is it ghosts from the water? Peer? Peer? Up there on the hill. (*She runs up a small hill and gazes over the tarn.*) Not a sign to be seen.

SOLVEIG'S FATHER: All the worst for him.

ÅSE: (*Crying*) Peer, lamb lost.

SOLVEIG'S FATHER: That's right, lost.

ÅSE: Don't talk like that. None like him. So fine, so handsome.

SOLVEIG'S FATHER: You foolish woman.

ÅSE: Yes, foolish, I am foolish, but my boy is all right.

SOLVEIG'S FATHER: His heart is hard, his soul is lost.

ÅSE: Never. Our Lord forgives.

SOLVEIG'S FATHER: Is he able to repent his sins?

ÅSE: No, but he can cut the air riding bucks –

SOLVEIG'S MOTHER: My God, are you mad?

ÅSE: Nothing he couldn't do. You'll see if he's just let live –

SOLVEIG'S FATHER: Better for you if you saw him hanging by the neck.

ÅSE: In the holy name of Jesus.

SOLVEIG'S FATHER: Leave him to Christ, he might repent.

ÅSE: Are you out to destroy me? We have to find him.

SOLVEIG'S FATHER: Save his soul.

ÅSE: Save his body. If the mountain magic's taken him, ring the bells in the church for him.

SOLVEIG'S FATHER: Here's the path for cattle.

ÅSE: God protect you for your help.

SOLVEIG'S FATHER: It's Christian duty.

ÅSE: Heathens, all the others. Was there one to go with us.

SOLVEIG'S FATHER: They knew him too well.

ÅSE: He was too good for them. (*She wrings her hands.*) Now think of it, his life in danger.

SOLVEIG'S FATHER: See the trace of a man's foot.

ÅSE: Search here.

SOLVEIG'S FATHER: We'll search below. (*He and his wife leave.*)

SOLVEIG: Tell me a bit more.

   (ÅSE *dries her eyes.*)

ÅSE: About my son?

SOLVEIG: Everything, yes.

   (ÅSE *smiles and bridles.*)

ÅSE: Everything? I'll wear you out.

SOLVEIG: Sooner you wear out talking than I will listening.

SCENE 3

Low treeless heights under the mountain plain. Further away, peaks are visible. It is late in the day, the time of shadows. PEER *runs at full speed, stopping on the slopes.*

PEER GYNT: This is better than a barney with the blacksmith. This is the life. I could kill a bear. (*He hits out, jumping in the air.*) Smash all before me, send it spinning. Stop water flowing, tear trees from the roots. This is the life. To hell with watery lies.

   (*Three mountain* GIRLS *run over the hills, singing and shouting.*)

GIRLS: Trolls of the Valfjell, Bard and Kare, sleep in our arms, will you, Trond?

FIRST GIRL: Trond, be gentle.

SECOND GIRL: Bard, be strong.

THIRD GIRL: The beds in the byres are cold.

FIRST GIRL: Strong is gentle.

SECOND GIRL: Gentle, strong.

THIRD GIRL: Where there's no lads, play with the trolls.

PEER GYNT: Where are the lads?

(*The* GIRLS *howl with laughter*.)

GIRLS: They're not let come.

FIRST GIRL: Mine would have courted me sweetheart and wife but now he's landed with a wrinkled widow.

SECOND GIRL: Mine met a tinker in the hills up north and now they're two of them tramps on the road.

THIRD GIRL: Mine killed our bastard and now his skull smiles at the world from the end of a stake.

GIRLS: Trolls of the Valfjell, Bard and Kare, sleep in our arms, will you, Trond?

(*With a leap* PEER GYNT *stands among them*.)

PEER GYNT: This troll has three heads, lad enough for three lassies.

GIRLS: Are you up to us?

PEER GYNT: Tell me when we've stopped.

FIRST GIRL: To the byre, the byre.

SECOND GIRL: We have drink.

PEER GYNT: Pour it into me.

THIRD GIRL: No cold beds this Saturday night.

SECOND GIRL: (*Kisses him*) He's like a hammer sprouting red hot iron.

THIRD GIRL: (*Kisses him*) Eyes like a baby's dipped deep in the water.

(PEER *dances among them*.)

PEER GYNT: Heart and mind, do your damnedest, the notion's rising in me. Eyes laugh, throat cry, the notion's rising in me.

(*The* GIRLS *thumb their noses to the peaks, shouting and singing*.)

GIRLS: Trolls of the Valfjell, Bard and Kare, sleep in our arms, will you, Trond?

(*They dance off together with* PEER GYNT.)

SCENE 4

Along the Rondane Mountains. It is sunset. Snowpeaks gleam all around.

PEER GYNT: That gate it's gleaming. Stand still, stand – it's fading further and further away. I can see birds and treetrunks like giants with heron's feet. They're fading away into rainbows that cut through my head. I've a pain there, burning red-hot – some devil's tied rings around me. (*He sinks down.*) The birds are on the move and here's me winding through muck to my knees. I'll fly with them. I'll clean myself in the waters of high minds. I'll raise myself. I'll leap into the holy christening font. I'll fly about the mountain fields. Soar the ocean and England's Emperor. Take a good look here, girls. No point waiting for me – well, I'll nip down maybe, now and then. Where are the mighty birds? Did the devil take them? Take them all. Look, a new house being built. The gable end rising, every corner growing, the very ground lifting, the gate wide open. Grandfather's new farm. Not a sign of rags nor fences falling. Every window pane shining. A big night in the great hall. The knives click against the glasses. The captain's bottle's flung against the mirrored wall. Crash. Let it be. Let it go. Waste and want – enough, mother. Who gives a damn when big John Gynt holds a party? Let it rip from the Gynt men. The captain wants his son and heir. Drink to my good health. Give us music, give us singing, give us judgement. Peer Gynt came from a great tribe and he will come to greatness. (PEER *runs forward. He goes head first into a rock and lies there.*)

SCENE 5

*A hillside with large, leafy trees. Stars glitter through the leaves.
Birds sing in the trees. A woman, dressed in green, walks along the
hillside.*

GREEN WOMAN: Is that the honest truth?
    (PEER *cuts his throat with his finger.*)
PEER GYNT: True as my name's Peer. True as you take my
    breath away. Will you have me? I can treat a woman well.
    Your hands won't touch work. Eat your fill till you're
    bursting. I won't touch a hair of your head.
GREEN WOMAN: Nor lay a finger on me?
PEER GYNT: How could I? King's sons don't beat their women.
GREEN WOMAN: Are you a king's son?
PEER GYNT: Yes.
GREEN WOMAN: My daddy's a king. The king of this mountain.
PEER GYNT: Is he?
GREEN WOMAN: Inside the mountain he has his palace.
PEER GYNT: As far as I know my ma's is bigger.
GREEN WOMAN: Do you know my father? He's called King
    Brose.
PEER GYNT: You might know my mother. Queen Åse?
GREEN WOMAN: When Daddy's cross, the mountains open.
PEER GYNT: When my ma gets going, the mountains fall.
GREEN WOMAN: When he's dancing, Daddy can leap to the
    roof.
PEER GYNT: My ma can paddle her way through the fastest
    river.
GREEN WOMAN: Do you have nothing but rags to dress up in?
PEER GYNT: You should take a look at my Sunday suit.
GREEN WOMAN: Even during the week I walk about in silk and
    gold.
PEER GYNT: Looks to me like a sack tied with straw.

GREEN WOMAN: You should remember one thing. We have our own ways here in the mountains. Nothing's what it seems, everything's its opposite. When you enter my father's court, you might easily believe you're standing in a heap of rubble.

PEER GYNT: Exactly the same with us. When you see our gold you might think it rubbish. Every glittering window pane, full of rags and stockings.

GREEN WOMAN: Black can be white and foul be fair.

PEER GYNT: Big can be small and dirty dainty.

(*She falls on his neck.*)

GREEN WOMAN: Peer, we're two of a kind. We were made for each other.

PEER GYNT: Like the legs in my trousers and the hair in your comb.

(*She calls towards the hill.*)

GREEN WOMAN: Bring forward my bridal carriage.

(*An enormous pig comes running with a piece of rope for its bridle and an old sack for saddle.* PEER GYNT *mounts it, setting her before him.*)

Would you believe just now I was heartbroken? Who knows what can happen in this life?

(PEER *whips the pig as they trot off.*)

SCENE 6

The court of the mountain king. Fantastic creatures surround the building. There is great commotion.

TROLLS: Crucify him. Christ's son has bedded the king's beautiful daughter.

FIRST CHILD: Can I slice his finger off?

SECOND CHILD: Can I eat his hair?

GIRL: Can I bite his arse?

(*The* TROLL WITCH *shakes a ladle.*)

27

WITCH: Let me strip into soup and flesh.

(*The* SECOND WITCH *has a carving knife.*)

SECOND WITCH: Roast him red, spit him in a pot.

KING: Cool yourselves, ice your blood.

(*He beckons his confidants near.*)

No time for bragging. These past few years we've been on our uppers. This boy here, I know he's human, but we need a hand, this one's spotless. Power of strength in it from what I see. I know, I know, he has only one head, but my daughter's no better endowed. This fad for three heads is on the way out. You rarely see a troll with two heads, and even then, it's hard to believe.

(*He speaks to* PEER GYNT.)

Is it my daughter you're after? Out there, beneath this beautiful mountain, I hear it's said, this above all, man, to thine own self be true, but inside here, among the pack that's in it, we say, to your own self be your self alone.

TROLL: Do you follow him?

KING: Yourself alone, my boy, your precious own. Let it be the way the world knows you.

(PEER *scratches his ear.*)

PEER GYNT: Well, I –

KING: You must, if you want to lord it here.

PEER GYNT: All right, but Christ, I don't know.

KING: We're the salt of the earth. Can you make yourself at home among simple folk?

(*He beckons two trolls with pig's heads and white nightcaps.*)

Bring us meat and drink. Our cows shit cakes and the bulls piss wine. Sour or sweet, no matter, isn't it homemade?

(PEER *pushes it away.*)

PEER GYNT: Hell's gates to your homebrew. I'll never get used to your ways here.

KING: The bowl goes with it. Pure gold. Who owns the gold owns my daughter.

(PEER GYNT *thinks.*)

PEER GYNT: Well, they say control your urges. In the long run the drink may sweeten. Hand it here.

KING: Sensible man. Tell me, do you spit?

PEER GYNT: Every man to his own habits.

KING: Now, throw off those Christian clothes. It's the pride and joy of the mountain people here that everything's homemade. Not a stitch from those beyond us, except the silk bow at the tip of your tail.

PEER GYNT: I haven't got a tail.

KING: We can provide. Fetch my tail, my Sunday best, tie it on him.

PEER GYNT: You will not. Do you want me to look like a lunatic?

KING: Don't court my daughter wearing a bare arse.

PEER GYNT: Would you turn me into a beast?

KING: Son dear, you're far mistaken. I want to fashion you into a good catch. A bright yellow bow, that's your livery. Here it's looked on as the highest honour.

PEER GYNT: They say unto dust we do return, so why worry against fashion? Tie away.

KING: Good man, good man.

TROLL: Let's see how well you wag your tail.

PEER GYNT: What more do you want? My faith in Christ?

KING: You're welcome to keep it. Faith's for nothing here. A troll's known by the cut of his coat. Manners make the man in these parts. Keep your faith, it's only fear.

PEER GYNT: You drive a hard bargain but you're a reasonable man.

KING: The troll's bark is worse than his bite – another difference between us and you. Enough philosophy. Girls, delight our eyes and ears. Girls, come out and shake a leg. (*Music and dance.*)

TROLL: What do you make of it?

PEER GYNT: What do I make –

KING: Speak your mind. What do you see?

PEER GYNT: Something to make your stomach sick.

TROLLS: Cut him. Skin him. Eat him without salt.

KING: Easy, easy.

TROLLS: Knife his ears off.

KING: He's only human.

TROLLS: Rip out his eyes.

KING: They're all he sees with.

(*The* GREEN WOMAN *cries.*)

GREEN WOMAN: Have me and my sister to put up with such abuse when we're entertaining?

PEER GYNT: Oh, was it you? A slag between friends can be kindly meant, you know.

GREEN WOMAN: Do you swear to that?

PEER GYNT: Great singing, lovely dancing, cat tear my eyes out if I lie.

KING: Humanity's a funny thing. It goes on and on. Us and them, we're in a scrap, we leave a mark, but it heals quickly. This son-in-law is easygoing. He throws off his Christian drawers. Downs the quick drop of drink, wagging the tail he ties to his arse. Whatever he's asked, he does, so you'd think he'd lost his Father Adam. But look, he has the upper hand. Well, boyo, you need treatment to cure this dangerous humanity.

PEER GYNT: What'll you do?

KING: Scratch a bit out of your left eye first. All things bend. The world rights itself. Then a bit out of your right eye –

PEER GYNT: Are you drunk?

(*The* KING *places some sharp instruments on the table.*)

KING: Have you ever watched them cutting glass? We'll blinker you like a mad bull. Then the bride is beauty itself. No more pigs dancing or cows playing.

PEER GYNT: This is madman's talk.

OLD TROLL: It's the talk of a king. He's sane, you're mad.

KING: Think of the bother you're saving yourself. That eye of yours. It sees sorrow. The source of all sorrow.

PEER GYNT: True enough, and they say in the Bible, if your eye offends, pluck it out. If I do it, will I ever see the world again?

KING: Never, my friend.

PEER GYNT: Then thanks but no thanks.

KING: Where are you going?

PEER GYNT: Out.

KING: Halt. The way in here is easily found, but the way out is no way out.

PEER GYNT: Are you going to keep me here by force?

KING: Listen, Peer, be sensible, prince. You have the makings of a troll. A gift for it, you might say. You're halfway there, already, I might say. Isn't it what you want to be?

PEER GYNT: By Christ, I do. Throw in a bride and a tidy kingdom, I'll give up half the human race. But there's limits. It's true I wear the tail and threw off the trousers, but I can pull them on again and sail away from mountain life. Do you want me to swear the cow's a bride? Right you be, for now I'll swallow the swearing. But chain myself and wander my days with you, never to die? No. It's written in the book that a man must die – so what you want is something I won't give you.

KING: Don't play with me, you white-faced pup. Do you know who I am?

PEER GYNT: You're a lying mouth.

KING: You have to marry her.

PEER GYNT: Are you accusing me?

KING: What of? Can you deny lusting for her?

PEER GYNT: Is that all? Who gives a damn –

KING: All the same, humans. You know about your soul's desire, but you only value what's in your grab. Does lust count for nothing, you think? Wait, you'll learn different.

GREEN WOMAN: Peer love, you'll be a daddy before the year's over.

PEER GYNT: Let me out, let me out.

31

KING: I'll send the bastard to you wrapped in a goat's skin.

(PEER *wipes his brow.*)

PEER GYNT: Let me wake up.

KING: Shall we send him to your palace?

PEER GYNT: Send him to your poorhouse.

KING: All right, Prince Peer, that's your concern. One thing's certain though. What's done is done. Your seed's sown and bad weed grows fast.

PEER GYNT: Old man, don't charge at me like a bull. Lady, be reasonable. Face facts. I'm neither prince nor plenty. Take me what way you want me. You'll gain nothing by having me.

(*The* GREEN WOMAN *throws a fit. She is carried out by troll girls. The* KING *looks at* PEER *with total contempt. He speaks.*)

KING: My children? Do you see the rocks? Smash him to pieces.

CHILD: Father? Turn him into an owl and me into an eagle.

SECOND CHILD: Play wolf.

THIRD CHILD: Play cat and mouse.

KING: All these things, but quickly. I am cross. I am sleepy. Goodnight.

(*He goes.* PEER *is chased by troll children.*)

PEER GYNT: Devils. Leave me alone. (*He tries to get up the chimney.*)

MALES: Sisters.

FEMALES: Brothers.

MALES: Get his arse.

FEMALES: His arse, his arse.

OLD TROLL: Our young are having fun.

(PEER *fights off a young troll who has bitten into his ear.*)

PEER GYNT: Let go of me, bastard.

(*The* OLD TROLL *raps* PEER's *knuckles.*)

OLD TROLL: Respect your royal betters. Be gentle with the child.

(PEER *runs to a rat-hole.*)

PEER GYNT: Rat. Rat-hole. Rat.

MALES: Sisters.

FEMALES: Brothers.

MALES: Cut him.

FEMALES: Off. Cut him.

MALES: Off. Cut.

PEER GYNT: Their father –

FEMALES: Cut him.

PEER GYNT: Be damned.

MALES: Cut him.

PEER GYNT: His young –

FEMALES: Cut him.

PEER GYNT: Be fucked.

MALES: Lock him in.

FEMALES: Lock him up.

PEER GYNT: Turn me into a rat.

MALES: His eyes.

PEER GYNT: Turn me into vermin.

FEMALES: His eyes.

PEER GYNT: Mama.

MALES: His eyes.

PEER GYNT: Help me. (*He is buried in a pack of trolls.*)

FEMALES: His eyes.

PEER GYNT: I'm dying.

    (*Churchbells ring in the distance.*
    Silence.)

MALES: The mountains.

FEMALES: Bells.

MALES: The beasts.

FEMALES: Black beasts.

PEER GYNT: Mother.

MALES: Priests.

PEER GYNT: Wife.

FEMALES: Priests.

TROLLS: Black beasts, black beasts.
   (*The* TROLLS *run away*.)

SCENE 7

Pitch black. PEER GYNT *beats around the blackness with a large branch. A* VOICE, *the Great Boyg, sounds.*

PEER GYNT: Tell me, who are you?
VOICE: Who are you?
PEER GYNT: I can go round –
VOICE: Go round.
PEER GYNT: Out of the way.
VOICE: Go the round way.
PEER GYNT: Who are you?
VOICE: You?
PEER GYNT: Can you say –
VOICE: Can you say.
PEER GYNT: What I like. This is a sword. It can kill, watch
   yourself. Stop this stupidity. Who are you?
   (*Silence.*)
   (*Speech marked within brackets is simultaneous.*)
PEER GYNT: Don't think I don't know. Out of my way.
VOICE: My way. Go the round way.
PEER GYNT: I will fight my way through.
VOICE: Peer.
PEER GYNT: Is there more than one of you?
VOICE: More than one of you.
PEER GYNT: Who are you?
VOICE: Who are you?
PEER GYNT: Peer Gynt.
VOICE: Peer Gynt.
PEER GYNT: Only one.
VOICE: Only one.
PEER GYNT: Safe.

34

VOICE: Safe.
(PEER GYNT: Sure.
VOICE: Sure.
PEER GYNT: Dead.
VOICE: Dead.
PEER GYNT: Alive.
VOICE: Alive.)
  (PEER *throws down the branch*.)
PEER GYNT: It's cursed. I have my fists. Body.
VOICE: Body.
PEER GYNT: I am (Peer Gynt.
VOICE: Peer Gynt.)
PEER GYNT: Reach (forth.
VOICE: Forth, there I am.
PEER GYNT: There I am. There.
VOICE: There.) Around the corner.
PEER GYNT: Corner. (I am
VOICE: I am outside.
PEER GYNT: Outside.) In the middle.
VOICE: Middle. (Name –
PEER GYNT: Name yourself.
VOICE: Yourself.)
PEER GYNT: Let me see you.
VOICE: You.
PEER GYNT: What are you?
  (*Silence*.)
PEER GYNT: Not dead.
VOICE: Dead.
PEER GYNT: Not alive.
VOICE: Alive.
PEER GYNT: Mad.
VOICE: Not mad.
PEER GYNT: Fight.
VOICE: No fight.
PEER GYNT: You shall fight.

(*Silence.*)

PEER GYNT: Nothing.

VOICE: Nothing.

PEER GYNT: You.

VOICE: You.

PEER GYNT: Conquer nothing.

VOICE: Nothing.

    (PEER *bites his own hands and arms.*)

PEER GYNT: I am tearing claw and tooth and my flesh is blood.

    (*There is the loud sound of birds' wings.*)

BIRDCRY: Is he coming?

VOICE: Coming.

BIRDCRY: My sisters, time to meet.

PEER GYNT: Save me, girl. Quick. Don't look down so modest.

    The prayerbook, hurl it into his eyes.

BIRDCRY: His eyes.

VOICE: His eyes.

BIRDCRY: Sisters, see his eyes.

PEER GYNT: Let this hour of torture end this life.

BIRDCRY: He's fallen. Take him.

VOICE: Take him.

    (*Bells ring. Hymns are sung in the distance.*)

BIRDCRY: Strong, he's strong.

VOICE: Strong.

    (*The* HYMN *sings.*)

HYMN: Lord, born of woman –

VOICE: Woman.

HYMN: We stand behind him safely –

VOICE: Woman. Strong. Behind him.

SCENE 8

It is sunrise. The mountains. PEER GYNT *lies asleep outside the
hut's well. He wakes up slowly and spits.*

PEER GYNT: What I'd do for a fresh herring. (*He spits again, seeing* HELGA.) Hi, you, what are you here for? What do you want?

HELGA: Solveig.

(*He jumps up.*)

PEER GYNT: Where is she?

HELGA: Hiding behind the wall.

SOLVEIG: Come near me and I'll run away.

PEER GYNT: Are you afraid I'll give you a squeeze?

SOLVEIG: Mind your manners.

PEER GYNT: Do you know where I was last night? I'm being chased by the mountain king's daughter.

SOLVEIG: Then thank God church bells were rung.

PEER GYNT: Peer Gynt's no man to be easily led, would you agree?

(HELGA *cries out.*)

HELGA: She's run away.

(*Runs after her*) Wait.

PEER GYNT: (*Grabs* HELGA'*s arm*) Wait and see what I've in my pocket. A silver button. I'll give it to you, pet, if you put in a good word for me.

HELGA: Let me go.

PEER GYNT: There it is.

HELGA: Let me go. Here's the food basket.

PEER GYNT: God help you, if you don't –

HELGA: You frighten me.

PEER GYNT: No. (*He lets her go. He is meek now.*) I beg you, let her not forget me.

(HELGA *runs away.*)

ACT THREE

SCENE I

The pineforest. It is autumn. The snow falls. In his shirt-sleeves PEER
GYNT *fells timber. He chops at a large fir with gnarled branches.*

PEER GYNT: Well, for an old man, you're tough. Much good it'll
do you. You're about to get the chop. (*He chops the tree.*) I
can see it's a suit of armour, but it's for piercing, no matter
how tough. Go on, shake your wrinkled fist. Come what
may, you'll be left on your knees. (*He breaks off suddenly.*)
Lies. Only an old tree. Lies. Not an ancient knight. Only a
fir tree, the bark cracked. Hard work, cutting timber. Hell's
work, dreaming as you're cutting. Stop this, standing
dreaming, my eyes wide open in the fog. You're out of
order, boy. Into the forest with you. That's your
banishment. It's official. (*He chops the tree vigorously.*) Out of
bounds, yes indeed. No ma to dish up grub and set the
table. Woman yourself about the house. Build a house?
Then quarry stone. A house of wood? Bear it on your back
to the door. (*The axe sinks down. He looks in front of him.*)
Mighty. Mighty workmanship. Look at the roof, like a
tower and spire. Last touch, on the gable, look, a woman
from the sea shaped like a fish beneath. Brass on the locks.
Get me glass. Outsiders will wonder what's shining from the
hillside. (*Annoyed, he laughs.*) Lies, damned lies. You're out
of order, boy. (*He chops vigorously. Suddenly he stands still,
listening, the axe raised.*) Someone's after me. Ingrid's old
fella? (*Getting down behind the tree, he peeps out.*) It's a young
fella. On his own. He seems scared, looking all around him.
What's that hidden under his cart? A sickle. He's stopped.
He's stopped. He's put his hand on the fence. What is it?
Why is he steadying himself? What is it? Christ. He's
chopped off his finger. The whole finger. He's bleeding like

38

a bull. He's up and running with a cloth round his hand. (*He gets up.*) That's some devil. A good finger cut completely. Nobody forced him – yes, now I understand. That's the only way to miss the king's shilling. That's it. They were sending him off to war. So the lad, could you blame him, wouldn't go, but chop – off forever – yes, think it, wish it – want it even, that I understand – but *do* it – do it – do it – (*He shakes his head a little, then goes back to work.*)

SCENE 2

Åse's house. A room. Everything is in disorder. Chests have fallen open, clothes everywhere. ÅSE *and* KARI *busy themselves packing and putting things in place.* ÅSE *goes to one side of the room.*

ÅSE: Kari, listen here.

KARI: What?

ÅSE: Listen. Where is? Where will I find? Answer me where? What am I looking for? Am I going mad? Where is the key to the closet?

KARI: In the keyhole?

ÅSE: (*Cries*) What a body is put through. God in his mercy help me. The whole house cleared. They pulled the very stitch from my back. (*She spits.*) Christ scald them for their hard hearts. (*She sits down on the edge of the bed.*) We've lost family farm and land. The old Hagstead farmer was hard, but the law was harder. Neither help nor mercy from them. I had nobody. Peer was gone.

KARI: At least you've your home till you die.

ÅSE: Me and the cat, aye, chewing the crumbs of charity.

KARI: God love you, woman, Peer's cost you plenty.

ÅSE: Peer? Are you off your head? Didn't Ingrid get home safely? Would the two of them run off to hell's gates? The devil led my lad astray.

KARI: Should I send word to the priest? Things must be worse than you believe.

ÅSE: Priest? Maybe so, yes. (*She stands up.*) Damned if I do. Am I not the boy's mother? I'll help him. What else is my duty? Make the best of it. Let the rest of them give up on him. They've left him this jacket. Would to God I'd dared pinch the fur rug. Where are the socks?

KARI: There, in the other rubbish.

(ÅSE *scrabbles around.*)

ÅSE: Kari, look, the old ladle. He used play with it. Pretend he was a buttonmoulder. Melt and shape and stamp. And one big night the child came in and asked his father for a lump of tin. No tin, John said, but the king's portrait. Silver. Let the world see you are John Gynt's son. God forgive John, but he was drunk and paid heed to neither gold nor tin. Here's the socks full of holes. They need darning, Kari.

KARI: You can certainly say that.

ÅSE: When I've that done, I'll take myself to bed. I'm not well at all at all. (*She grows happy.*) The woollen shirts, Kari. They've missed them.

KARI: Right enough, so they have.

ÅSE: Luck's with us. Throw one aside. Listen, we'll take the two. The one he's wearing is worn out.

KARI: God spare us, Åse, that's a sin.

ÅSE: I suppose so, but sure God forgives sins.

SCENE 3

A newly built cabin in the wood. Snow is piled up high. It is twilight. Standing outside the door, PEER GYNT *fastens a large wooden lock. He laughs occasionally.*

PEER GYNT: There must be a lock that bars the house against trolls and against men and women. There must be a lock that can shut out all the crabbed whispering. At night they come here, beating against the door. Open up, Peer Gynt, we're in your head. We're under your bed. We rake the ashes. Do you see us glowing like dragons up the chimney? Do you think wood and nail can stop the whisperers?

(SOLVEIG *comes on skis over the heath. She has a shawl over the head and a bundle in her hand.*)

SOLVEIG: God bless the work. Don't turn on me. I came as sent for, so take me.

PEER GYNT: Solveig? Are you not frightened to come near me?

SOLVEIG: Helga brought your message. The wind and the calm carried others. Everything your mother told me spoke the same story. Through the long nights and the empty days I heard I must come. Down below there it was like life had died. My heart could neither laugh nor cry. I didn't know where you stood. I only knew what I had to do.

PEER GYNT: Your father?

SOLVEIG: As God is my judge I have nobody, neither Father nor Mother. I've turned my back on them all.

PEER GYNT: Solveig, you dove, have you come to me?

SOLVEIG: Yes, you alone. You have to be my all, my friend, my comfort. (*She weeps.*) It was hard to let go of my little sister. Harder to part from Father. Hardest of all to leave the one that birthed me. No. God forgive me, the sorest sorrow is to be parted from them all. All.

PEER GYNT: You know what sentence the court passed. I've neither land nor money.

SOLVEIG: Did money or land drive me away from the ones I hold dearest?

PEER GYNT: Do you know if I'm found outside the forest, anyone may seize me?

SOLVEIG: I asked my way here. They wondered where I was going. I told them. Home.

PEER GYNT: Then to hell with wood and nails. To hell with devils whispering. With you beside this man, I know the house is holy. Let me look at you, Solveig. Not too near. Just want to look at you. Pure beauty. Let me lift you. Beautiful. Delicate. Let me carry you, Solveig, and I'll never tire. I won't stain you, I'll stretch out my arms and hold you away from me. You're warm. Who would have thought I could have drawn your beauty here? I've longed for you night and day. Look here, I've cut timber and built this. It will fall down, love, it's ugly, it's poor –

SOLVEIG: Rich or poor, here's my heart's peace. Breath comes easy in the sweeping wind. Down there it was like suffocating. I think that frightened me out of the valley. Here the fir trees sing – it's still, the singing. Here is home.

PEER GYNT: Are you certain? For the rest of your life?

SOLVEIG: I've chosen my path. It doesn't turn round.

PEER GYNT: Then I have you. Go inside. Let me see you in the house. I'll fetch wood for the fire. I'll make it warm and snug. I'll light a big fire. You'll sit at your ease and never feel the cold. (*He opens the door.*)

(SOLVEIG *goes in.* PEER *stands still, then laughs loudly, jumping in the air.*)

Gentle, gentle woman, mine. Found and won. The palace will rise from the ground. (*He takes the axe and walks along.*)

(*An oldish woman, wearing a tattered green skirt, comes out. An ugly brat with a beermug in his hand follows her, limping, clinging to her skirts.*)

WOMAN: Good evening, Mister Hotheels.

PEER GYNT: What? Who's there?

WOMAN: Old pals, Peer Gynt. My house is near. We're related.

PEER GYNT: That's news to me.

WOMAN: As you built your house, so did mine build itself.

PEER GYNT: I'm in a bit of a hurry.

WOMAN: Aren't you always, boy? Never mind, I'll toddle after you. We'll meet up in the end.

PEER GYNT: Lady, you're making a mistake.

WOMAN: I made that before this. I made that when you made your big promise.

PEER GYNT: Promise? What the hell kind of talk –

WOMAN: Have you forgotten you sat drinking one night with my father? Have you forgotten –

PEER GYNT: How can I forget what I never knew? What are you rambling about? When did we last meet?

WOMAN: Last time we met was the first time. Give your daddy a drink. He looks thirsty.

PEER GYNT: Daddy? Are you drunk? Do you call him –

WOMAN: Can you not recognize a pig by its skin? Have you got eyes? Do you not see, he's as twisted in the hip as you in your soul.

PEER GYNT: Are you saying – ?

WOMAN: Are you worming out of it?

PEER GYNT: That long-legged brat?

WOMAN: He grew up quick.

PEER GYNT: Listen, witchface, are you pointing the finger –

WOMAN: No, you listen, Peer, roaring like a bull at me. (*She cries.*) Is it my fault I lost the looks I had when you'd your way with me? I gave birth last autumn and the devil grabbed me by the belly. Is it a wonder I'm ugly? Do you want me beautiful? Then show the girl in there the road. Chase her out of sight and mind. Do that, dear friend, and I'll lose the snout.

PEER GYNT: Get out of my sight, witch.

WOMAN: Never will I.

PEER GYNT: I'll kick your skull in.

WOMAN: I dare you try. No, Peer Gynt, I can take a kick. Every blessed day I'll be back. You'll be sitting with her, making eyes, playing footsie, but I'll claim my rights. Her and me, we'll bargain for you. Farewell, sweet boy, you can marry tomorrow.

PEER GYNT: I've dreamt you from hell.

WOMAN: One thing's certain though. Have the brat. Raise him, you wandering good-for-nothing. Do you want to go with your daddy, little demon?

BRAT: Damn him.

(*The* BRAT *spits at* PEER.)

Give me the axe. I'll kill. Just wait. Just wait.

(*The* WOMAN *kisses the* BRAT.)

WOMAN: Look at the fine head on his shoulders. You'll be the spitting image of your father when you're a man.

(PEER *stamps his foot.*)

PEER GYNT: Would you were as far away –

WOMAN: As we're now near?

(PEER *wrings his hands.*)

PEER GYNT: It's come to this –

WOMAN: Because you imagined your desire. I pity you, Peer, it's hard lines.

PEER GYNT: Harder for another. I have gold, Solveig, pure, no hand touched her.

WOMAN: Aye, it's the innocent suffer, or so weeps the devil.

(*She plods into the trees with the* BRAT.)

(*He throws the beer mug at* PEER. *There is a long silence.*)

PEER GYNT: Go the round way, the voice said in the darkness. And here I have to do that. The palace falls. It's grown ugly here. My joy's aged. Maybe there's something to be done. Something like penance, if I remember right, but what? I've forgotten most of it, what the good book says, but where's there instruction in this wild forest? Penance? Maybe it would take years before I won through. What's the worth of such a life? Surely it was a lie about the hag's snout. That pretty picture is out of sight – out of sight, yes, not out of mind. Bad thoughts hound me. Ingrid and the three mountain lassies, will they do their bit too? Come laughing and shouting if they see her on my knee? Wanting my arms to open for them tender and gently. Go the round way. See that pine, see that fir, would my arm were as long – I can never hold her tightly without harming – dirtying –

how do I get round this and neither win nor woe? Get such things out of your head. Forget it ever happened. (*He walks towards the hut but stops.*) How can I go in after this? I'm ugly, I'm soiled. There's something evil in my company. Tomorrow's a holy day. Were I to meet her now, it would be sacrilege.

(SOLVEIG *stands in the doorway.*)

SOLVEIG: Are you coming?

PEER GYNT: Go the round way.

SOLVEIG: What?

PEER GYNT: Wait. It's dark. I've something heavy to fetch.

SOLVEIG: I'll give you a hand. We'll share the load.

PEER GYNT: No, hold your ground. I've to carry it all.

SOLVEIG: Don't go too far, love.

PEER GYNT: Patience, girl. Far or near, you'll have to wait.

SOLVEIG: Yes, I'll wait.

(PEER GYNT *walks along the forest path.* SOLVEIG *stands in the open door.*)

SCENE 4

Åse's room. Evening. A log fire burns, lighting the chimney. KARI *sits on a chair at the foot of the bed.* ÅSE *lies in bed, fumbling restlessly with the bedspread.*

ÅSE: Sweet God, is he not coming? Why's it taking so long? I can't get him word, and there's so much to say. We haven't time to waste. It passes so quickly. Who'd have thought? If I only knew I hadn't been too strict with him.

PEER GYNT: (*Enters*) Good evening to you.

ÅSE: God bless you, you're here, my own son. How did you face coming down here? Do you not know they'd take your life here?

PEER GYNT: Forget about my life. I'm here to see you.

ÅSE: Kari can hide her head in shame. I can go in peace.

45

(KARI *leaves the room.*)

PEER GYNT: Go? Where? What are you saying?

ÅSE: Son, the end's come. I've little time left.

(PEER *shakes and walks through the room.*)

PEER GYNT: Yes, well, I ran away from suffering, here I thought I might be rid . . . Your hands and feet, are you cold?

ÅSE: Yes, Peer. It soon goes. Close them gently when you see my eyes glass over. Find a coffin, let it be a strong one. No, I forgot –

PEER GYNT: Calm. Time enough to think about that.

ÅSE: Yes, yes. (*She looks about the room restlessly.*) Have you seen the little left us? Isn't that their like?

(PEER *is nervous.*)

PEER GYNT: Are you at it again? (*He speaks harshly.*) It's my fault, I know. What good comes of being reminded of it?

ÅSE: Not your fault. Drink's fault. A curse. Son dear, you were drunk. You didn't know what you were doing. You'd ridden the big buck. It's to be expected you were wild.

PEER GYNT: Let that yarn pass. Let it all pass. Save whatever brings bother to another day. (*He sits on the edge of her bed.*) Ma, we'll talk about this and that between us. Forget what's bitter and sore. So, what's the gossip?

ÅSE: (*Smiling*) I hear there's a girl round here who's always looking up to the mountains.

PEER GYNT: Mads Moen, has he settled down?

ÅSE: I hear that her people cry and she doesn't hear them. Have a look in there, Peer, you might cure –

PEER GYNT: Aslak the smith, where's he ended up?

ÅSE: Forget about that dirty thing. I'd rather tell you her name, the girl, you know –

PEER GYNT: Let whatever's bitter pass. Are you dry? Will I fetch you a drink? Can you stretch yourself out? This bed's short. Let me see. God, is this the bed I slept in as a boy?

Do you remember sitting on the edge of my bed, tucking the blankets about me, singing old songs?

ÅSE: And do you remember letting on we were going for rides on the sleigh when your daddy was travelling far away? The floor was all water iced over and there was a fur rug covering the sleigh.

PEER GYNT: Ma, do you remember best of all the beautiful horses?

ÅSE: Don't you know I do? We borrowed Kari's cat. Sat it on the big chair.

PEER GYNT: There is a palace in the moon
    And a palace in the sun,
    And to Santa Maria Palace
    All roads are said to run.

(*Silence.*)

Remember finding a stick in the press? You used it like a whip handle.

ÅSE: Me, sitting in the front seat, proud as punch, head high.

PEER GYNT: I mind you loosening the rein and turning round to ask if I was cold. Poor Ma, God love you, your soul was good. You're lamenting, why?

ÅSE: At my back, a hard board.

PEER GYNT: Stretch yourself. I'll hold you now. There, you're lying easier, there.

(ÅSE *is restless.*)

ÅSE: No, Peer, I want to leave.

PEER GYNT: Leave?

ÅSE: Leave. That's what I wish.

PEER GYNT: Nonsense. Pull the blanket round you. Let me sit on the edge of the bed. We'll kill the time singing.

ÅSE: Better fit to get the missal from the press. My mind's not at rest.

PEER GYNT: The King in Santa Maria
    With the prince shall dine.
    Recline on soft cushions,

                There will be time,
                There will be time.
ÅSE: But am I invited, Peer love?
PEER GYNT: Yes, we are, the two of us. (*He throws a piece of rope over the chair. Taking a stick in his hand, he sits in front at the foot of the bed.*) Gee up. Get a move on, Blackie. I hope you're not cold, Ma. You'll know you're travelling when this steed starts to move.
ÅSE: Peer, what's that ringing?
PEER GYNT: Sleighbells.
ÅSE: No, no, it's empty, it sounds empty.
PEER GYNT: Well, we're crossing the frozen water.
ÅSE: I'm afraid. What's that strange sigh rushing at me?
PEER GYNT: The trees talking to themselves, Ma. Sit still.
ÅSE: Something's glinting far away. I can see it blink. What is it, that gleam of light?
PEER GYNT: The palace windows, the glass doors. Can you hear them dancing?
ÅSE: Yes.
PEER GYNT: There's St Peter standing outside. He wants us to step inside.
ÅSE: Is he civil to us?
PEER GYNT: Very much so. He's pouring out sweet wine.
ÅSE: Why? Has he biscuits too?
PEER GYNT: A whole plateful. There's the bishop's dead wife. She's making coffee and dessert for you.
ÅSE: Goodness me, do we get on together?
PEER GYNT: Whatever you like, yes.
ÅSE: My goodness, this is some rejoicing you're treating me to, Peer, poor woman that I am.
                (PEER *cracks the whip.*)
PEER GYNT: Here the road's wide.
ÅSE: That quick pace. I feel sick and I'm tired.
PEER GYNT: I can see the palace rising. The drive will soon be over.

48

ÅSE: I'm in your hands, son.

PEER GYNT: Look at the crowds swarming and pushing to see Peer Gynt and his mother. What do you say, St Peter? My mother is not to be let in. Listen, you'll search high and low before you find a better soul. Forget about me. I want no entry unless you're offering a drink. I've spinned more yarns than the devil's preached from the pulpit. I've called my mother a clucking hen, but you treat her with respect. There's none better in this parish. Look out. Here comes the Boss. God the Father. You're for it now, St Peter. (*He speaks with a deep voice.*) Cut out acting the bouncer. Mother Åse, you're let in free. (*He laughs out loud, turning to his mother.*) See, didn't I tell you? He's changed his tune. (*He grows frightened.*) What's wrong with your eyes, Ma? Is something wrong? (*He goes to the top of the bed.*) Don't just lie there staring. Speak, Mama, it's me, your son. (*Tenderly he feels her forehead and hands. He throws the rope on to the chair and says softly*) Rest you now, journey's over. (*He shuts her eyes and bends over her.*) Thanks be to you for all your days. Your beatings and baby songs. Now thank me in return – (*He presses his cheek against her mouth.*) There. That was your thanks for the sleigh ride.

(KARI *enters.*)

KARI: What's wrong? Peer? Is the worst of the pain passed? Good God, she's sleeping sound, isn't she?

PEER GYNT: Ssssh, she's dead.

(KARI *cries by the corpse.* PEER GYNT *paces the room a long time, finally stopping by the bed.*)

See my mother gets a decent burial. I've to try and get away from here.

KARI: Will you go far away?

PEER GYNT: The sea?

KARI: That far?

PEER GYNT: Further. Further. (*He goes.*)

ACT FOUR

SCENE I

*Morocco. Palm trees. Dinner table set, sun blinds and rushmats.
Hammocks are tied further in among the trees. A steam yacht with
Norwegian and American flags, is moored offshore. A dinghy lies
beside the shore. It is approaching sunset.* PEER GYNT *presides as
host of the table. Middle-aged and handsome, he wears the elegant
travel clothes of a gentleman, with a gold lorgnette hanging from his
waistcoat.* COTTON, BALLON, VON EBERKOPF *and*
TRUMPETERSTRALE *are about to finish their meal.*

PEER GYNT: Gentlemen, drink. In pleasure are we created,
therefore pleasure we shall enjoy. What can I offer you?

TRUMPETERSTRALE: Super host, Gynt, super, quite, quite
super.

PEER GYNT: The honour is mine. My wealth, my cook, my
servant –

COTTON: Right on. I raise my glass to the health, to the
happiness of all four.

BALLON: *Monsieur*, you have a *gôut*, a *ton*, that in these days of
ours it is so rare, so rare to find, among men who live *en
garçon*, it is a certain, *je ne sais quoi, je ne peux dire quoi – je
ne* – I don't know.

EBERKOPF: I find it a feeling, an impression of a way of being
that is knowing of its place in the universe, and our stay
here is not long, but there is, there is a vision that touches
the clouds and breaks through them, a vision beyond,
beyond limit that gives a whole – a whole explanation to the
pristine quality of life, of experience in life which unites on
top of the triangle – the triangle of being, *Ja*?

BALLON: Quite. In French it is not so *élégant*.

EBERKOPF: *Ach*. That language is stiffy. So stiffy. But if we

want to seek, to elaborate, to unfold, to define – a reason
for this phenomenon –

PEER GYNT: We've found it. I never married. Gentlemen, the
meaning is clear. What shall a man be? Himself. That is
my short answer. He shall care for himself and his own.
Can he do this when he must burden himself like a camel
with other's woes, other's welfare?

EBERKOPF: Himself. *Ja*, himself. For one's self, to one's self. I
would promise it has cost you dearly – !

PEER GYNT: Yes. Yes indeed – long ago. However, I acquitted
myself with honour. There was one time I almost stepped
into the trap. Not my fault. Imagine me. A bright chap, a
handsome chap – she, the lady I, well, we know, she was of
Royal birth –

BALLON: Royal?

PEER GYNT: Family, family – you know – up there –

TRUMPETERSTRALE: (*Thumps the table*) Blood – blue blood –

PEER GYNT: (*Shrugs his shoulders*) Fur coat, no knickers – the
type who pride themselves that no Johnny is going to prick
their defences. Family crests against the proles, right?

COTTON: Your affair with this person, it didn't work out?

BALLON: The family disliked the match?

PEER GYNT: On the contrary.

BALLON: Ah.

PEER GYNT: Listen, men. Certain things, you follow, pushed us
in the direction of getting married, and getting married as
quickly as possible. But I speak my mind to you, you
know, the whole thing, from first to last, made me sick to
my stomach! Some things a chap sets his own standards on.
Stand up and be counted. The father, her father, creeps up
to me, suggests a change of name, change of outlook, join
the blue blood group. Usual shit and more, and I, with
grace, withdrew, laughed in his face and informed the
young – lady – to be gone. (*He bangs on the table and looks
pious.*) Yes, oh yes. There's a Fate we must follow, its will

decrees. That's all we humans can rely upon. But it's enough, and it's a comfort.

EBERKOPF: A good philosopher, like yourself, sees each of these seeds sown in so many directions as leading to the one end. You kept your standards. Every vague impression, every loose observation, you grasp as being the radiance of your world perception. Tell me, have you a BA?

PEER GYNT: Self-taught. I've told you. University of life. Thought, speculated, read up something on everything. No method but myself. Started too old, brain a little too weary to plough up and down through pages, taking in everything that moved. I've read a little history – no time for more. Religion? Bits and pieces – I believe now and then. I choose what I can use, practically –

COTTON: Now, that's what I call a believer.

PEER GYNT: (*Lights a cigar*) Friends, dear friends, take my life. How did I come to the West? I hadn't the arse in my trousers. I worked for a living, believe me, worked hard. But life is sweet, dear friends, and death is sour, they say. Fortune smiled on me, and fate was willing. It worked for me. I moved with the tide and it worked better and better. Do you know, ten years later the Charleston ship owners called me Croesus? My name went from port to port. Good fortune was my cargo –

COTTON: What did you carry?

PEER GYNT: Niggers to Carolina and dirty pictures to China.

BALLON: *Fi donc.*

TRUMPETERSTRALE: Heavens, dear Gynt.

PEER GYNT: Out of order, yes? I know, I felt the whole odious business weigh on me. But once you begin, once one begins, it's hard to stop. And I was giving employment. Get out of that one. But you know, there are consequences to all this, and the embarrassing thought struck me, who knows when my hour will come? What will the verdict be? Goats from sheep, separate them, when? There was a way

out, I found it. Every spring, the dirty pictures were duly
dispatched. Every autumn my missionaries followed suit. I
gave them what they required. Socks, bibles, rum, rice –

COTTON: Of course. And the profits?

PEER GYNT: Excellent. It worked. Coolies converted
everywhere.

COTTON: And the African – objects?

PEER GYNT: Morality, there too, got the better of me. When
one reaches a certain stage in life, it dawns on one that such
traffic may be wrong. Do-gooders, terrorists, wind and
weather, they can conspire. They won the day. I said,
Peter, call a halt, see the error of your ways. I bought a
little land in the south of Africa, saved the last herd –
slaves are meat – first-class meat – fed them up, leave them
fat and shining – it was a pleasure for me and them. I can
say this, yes, without boasting. I was like a father to them
and I got my reward. I built them schools, they learned
morality. They learned temperance. But I've got myself out
of it. Sold the plantation, sold the herd. Do you know, the
day I left, I gave them all, young and old, the cup that
cheers – free booze for men and women – get yourself
drunk – free snuff for all the widows.
(EBERKOPF *clinks glasses with him.* PEER GYNT *hits the
bottle.*)

EBERKOPF: I find it in my heart to lift when I meet a man of
principle.

PEER GYNT: I'm a Northerner. Northern men carry the war to
its bitter end. There is a way to lead one's life, an art one
might say. That art demands you close your ears to the
serpent's whisper.

COTTON: Dear friend, what serpent?

PEER GYNT: The little serpent who seduces you saying: 'Belong.
Belong.' (*Drinks again.*) But I say: 'Stand alone, with your
options open.' Life's a trap. Every day! Once more into the
breach, dear friends! but leave room to retreat. That's the

way forward. That's what shades and shapes it all. That's
my theory. That's the theory I was given. That's my past,
that's my people, that's my home.

BALLON: You are – !

PEER GYNT: That theory I inherited from my people in my
childhood home.

BALLON: Norwegian –

PEER GYNT: It has coloured all my behaviour, my conduct –

BALLON: You are Norwegian –

PEER GYNT: That theory has taken me forward.

BALLON: Aren't you Norwegian?

PEER GYNT: By birth?

   (*Silence*.)

   Yes. But I belong to the world, for that is my inclination. I
   have some fortune, for which I thank America. Germany's
   younger scholars, to them I owe my books. France gives
   me my waistcoats, my arrogance, my intellect – *un peu*.
   The Jews have taught me suffering, which some call
   patience, and others call learning, learning how to wait.
   And Italy has called me to sweet inclinations, *dolce far
   niente*.

TRUMPETERSTRALE: (*Lifts his glass*) *La dolce vita*!

   (*They touch glasses and drink to* PEER. *Peer's head is getting
   hot*.)

COTTON: Right on. Right, right on. But to business. Money.
   Your money. How will you use it?

   (*They draw closer*.)

CHORUS: Tell us.

COTTON: Where are you going? What's your aim?

PEER GYNT: Emperor.

CHORUS: What?

PEER GYNT: To be Emperor.

CHORUS: Where?

PEER GYNT: The world. Of the whole world.

BALLON: How, my friend?

54

PEER GYNT: Money. When I was a child it was my dream –
    Emperor – always there, like the ocean, like the clouds.
    Robed, golden, in dreams, and I'd wake up, but it was
    always there. They wrote somewhere, where I neither know
    nor remember, if you win the whole world and lose
    yourself, all you gain is a broken skull and a wreath to
    cover it. Gain the world and lose yourself.
EBERKOPF: This self, Peer Gynt, what is the self of Gynt?
PEER GYNT: In my head, behind my brow, there is a world
    which sees to it I am myself and no one else, as separate as
    God from the Devil.
TRUMPETERSTRALE: I understand the drift.
BALLON: Thinker. Sublime thinker.
EBERKOPF: Writer. Writer. Author. Author.
    (PEER GYNT's *spirit rises*.)
PEER GYNT: This self, Peer Gynt, which is the self of Gynt, it is
    an army, it wishes, it lusts, it desires. This self, Peer Gynt,
    oceans with ideas, whims, demands, it craves everything. It
    is this self that sees to it, I, as such, am alive. God needs
    dust to create. And I need gold to be Emperor.
BALLON: But you have gold.
PEER GYNT: Too little. Not enough to cram myself full from
    head to toe, so I may be Gynt of the whole world, Sir Gynt
    all the way through.
BALLON: (*Delighted*) Feel the finest women.
EBERKOPF: Drink the finest wine.
TRUMPETERSTRALE: The world's your oyster.
COTTON: Right on. But is there an opening for a little profit
    margin – ?
PEER GYNT: Already in the bag. That's why we dropped
    anchor. Tonight, we move north. The newspapers that
    came on board make interesting reading. (*He stands up, his
    glass raised*.) Fortune smiles unceasingly on those who help
    themselves.
CHORUS: Tell us.

PEER GYNT: The Greeks have risen up and rebelled.
   (*They all rise.*)
CHORUS: The Greeks?
PEER GYNT: Have revolted.
CHORUS: Hurrah.
PEER GYNT: Johnny Turk is in trouble. (*He empties his glass.*)
BALLON: Fair Greece. Let honour advance. My French weapons
   shall assist her.
COTTON: I can arrange delivery.
BALLON: (*Embraces* PEER GYNT) My friend, forgive me. I did
   not do you justice for a while.
EBERKOPF: (*Presses* PEER GYNT's *hand*) I am a dog, stupid, I
   took you for a cheat.
COTTON: Too strong. A fool, maybe.
TRUMPETERSTRALE: (*Would kiss* PEER GYNT) Old boy, I
   thought you were the lowest scum of Yankee – Shit.
   Forgive me.
EBERKOPF: We have all been horribly wrong.
PEER GYNT: What are you talking about?
EBERKOPF: Your wishes, your lusts, your desires, splendidly
   gathered here, the army of Peer Gynt.
   (BALLON *and* EBERKOPF *stand in admiration.*)
PEER GYNT: Look, tell me what –
BALLON: Do you not comprehend?
PEER GYNT: Hanged if I do.
BALLON: Are you not going to the Greeks with ships and
   money?
PEER GYNT: (*Shrugs*) No, thank you, I'm not. I'm with the
   stronger party. The Turk gets my money.
BALLON: Not possible.
EBERKOPF: Most witty, very witty, but a joke.
   (PEER GYNT *is silent for a while then leans against a chair and
   puts on a superior air.*)
PEER GYNT: Gentlemen, lend me your ears. Let us part as
   friends before we burn all our boats. When you own

nothing, it's easy to be daring. If you don't possess as much as your own shadow, then you're cut out for cannon fodder. But if you stand securely, as I do, on your own dry land, then the gamble is greater. *You* go to Greece. I'll send you armed men, all for free. You keep fuelling the fire, and I can better feed the flame. Liberty, equality – fight to the death for both. Make a hot hell for the Turk. End your life with honour, pinned to the end of a lance. I beg, however, to be excused. (*He pats his pocket.*) I am myself, Sir Peter Gynt, and I have money. (*He opens his parasol and walks into the copse where hammocks can be seen.*)

TRUMPETERSTRALE: Swine.

BALLON: Honour, blagh.

COTTON: Honour, God damn it, think of the profit that's in it for us if Greece freed itself.

BALLON: I saw myself, the hero, I saw a circle of Greek girls. Beautiful.

EBERKOPF: I saw the Fatherland, its great culture, spread all through the earth and sea –

COTTON: Goddamn, we've lost money, that's the kick in the balls. I could cry. I saw Mount Olympus, me its owner. There's copper in them there hills.

TRUMPETERSTRALE: We could still venture –

COTTON: Sure, into the middle of the scumbags where we put our heads into a noose. Where's the profit in that?

BALLON: *Merde.* So near to fortune, so far from –

COTTON: (*Raises his fist towards the ship*) In that coffinship Mr Bigshot sweats the gold from his niggers. That's where it is.

EBERKOPF: A good idea. That's it. His empire is there before us. Hurrah.

BALLON: What will you do?

EBERKOPF: Seize it. The crew can be bought easily. I shall possess the yacht.

COTTON: You what?

57

EBERKOPF: Thieve it. The lot. (*He goes down to the dinghy.*)
COTTON: It is, I assure you, purely my own interests which
    compel me to join the thieving. (*He goes after him.*)
TRUMPETERSTRALE: That's cheating.
BALLON: Terrible, terrible – but – *enfin!* (*He follows the others.*)
TRUMPETERSTRALE: Oh dear, I'd better toddle off with them,
    but under protest, under protest. (*He goes after them.*)

SCENE 2

*Another place on the coast. There is moonlight and drifting cloud.
The yacht goes at full speed, far out.* PEER GYNT *runs along the
shore. He pinches his arm, then looks out into the sea.*

PEER GYNT: A nightmare. I'll wake up. It's putting out to sea.
    It's not real. I'm asleep. I'm drunk. I'm mad. (*He wrings
    his hands.*) Can I be dying? (*He pulls his hair.*) It's a dream.
    I demand it to be a dream. No. Truth. Reality. Assholes.
    Asshole friends. Hear me, righteous Lord of wisdom. (*He
    raises up his arms.*) It's me, Peer Gynt. Lord, look on me.
    Father, protect me or I perish. Let them reverse the
    engine. Let them lower the gig. Stop the buggers. Heed
    me. Forget about other people. The world can look after
    itself for a while. I'm fucked if he's listening. (*He waves
    upwards.*) Hey, I let the plantation with the nigg – the
    negroes go. I sent my missionaries to Asia. I scratched your
    back, you scratch mine? Let me get on board.
    (*A flash of light shoots up from the yacht. Thick smoke pours
    out. A hollow bang sounds.* PEER GYNT *cries out and sinks
    down on the sand. Little by little the smoke clears. The ship has
    disappeared.*)
    (*Pale and quiet*) Rough justice. Rats and robbers to the
    bottom in one blow. Eternal praise to God's good luck. Just
    luck? No, more than that. I was destined to be saved and

they were to be destroyed. Praise be to you that guarded me, watched over me for all my faults. (*He breathes a sigh of relief.*) Isn't it wonderful to know you're singled out for protection? He's left me in the desert. Where do I get food and drink? What odds? I'll find something. He understands that. (*He speaks loudly and ingratiatingly.*) Would he let me, a poor little sparrow, starve? Give him time. The Lord will provide.

(*A lion roars. He starts up, frightened.*)

A lion, growling, was it in the rushes? (*His teeth clatter.*) No, never a lion.

(*Another roar.*)

It was a lion. Trust in the Lord. He gives me the bitter cup but he knows what I can bear to swallow. No more, no less than I am given. He's like a daddy to me, a father he is. But when it comes to money and managing it, you can forget it, God.

(*Another roar.*)

I wish I knew a couple of hymns.

(*He runs off.*)

SCENE 3

Night. A camp at the edge of the desert. A SLAVE *enters, tearing his hair.*

SLAVE: The horse, the horse, the Emperor's white horse.
Gone. Done a bunk. The horse.
(*An* OVERSEER *enters, tearing his clothes.*)
OVERSEER 1: Gone. Gone. The Emperor's holy vestments.
Stolen. Nicked. Robbed. Gone. The vestments.
(*Another* OVERSEER *enters.*)
OVERSEER 2: If one of yous come back here without catching
the bastard that ripped off the Emperor, yous will feel the

lash of the whip a hundred times on the soles of your feet
and I'm not messing.
(*The warriors gallop off in all directions.*)

SCENE 4

It is dawn. PEER GYNT, *a broken branch in his hand. He beats off
monkeys.*

PEER GYNT: Christ. A night to forget. (*He beats around.*)
(*The monkeys hurl shit.*)
That monkey is an animal. Disgusting.
(*More shit.*)
PEER GYNT: Leave off this nonsense.
(*A monkey approaches* PEER. *They exchange glances.* PEER
keeps still. The monkey moves. PEER *entices him coaxingly,
speaking lowly as if it were a dog.*)
PEER GYNT: Good boy, good boy, don't throw, no, of course
not, it's me, cuckoo, good pal. (PEER *screeches.*) See, I
know your language. Good boy, aren't we related? Sweeties
for you tomorrow.
(*The monkey throws the dirt over* PEER.)
PEER GYNT: The brute. The whole shebang on top of me.
Rotten. Wait a minute, is it food? (PEER *eats the dirt.*) Can't
make out the taste. Still, when it comes to taste, habit's
what counts.
(*The monkeys throw again.*)
PEER GYNT: (*Beats about the air*) I am Man, Lord of Creation, –
Damn you, damn all.
(*Exit, pursued by monkeys.*)

SCENE 5

*It is early morning. The country is stony with a view over the desert.
At one side there is a mountain gully and a cave. In the gully a thief*

60

and a receiver stand with the Emperor's horse and clothes. The horse is tethered to a stone. In the distance, horsemen are heard.

THIEF: I can feel the lance's tongues, licking me, playing with me.

RECEIVER: I can see my head rolling along the sand, oh, oh.

(*The* THIEF *folds his arms across his breast.*)

THIEF: My father thieved, so must I.

RECEIVER: My father received, so do I.

THIEF: Endure what's granted, be yourself.

RECEIVER: Footsteps. Where do we run?

THIEF: The cave is deep, and the prophet is good.

(*They flee, leaving the horse and clothes. Horsemen fade away in the distance.* PEER GYNT *enters.*)

PEER GYNT: Did God intend to create this graveyard? No sign of life, dried up, no use to anybody. A corpse since the day of birth that never smiled at its mother. Why was it created? Is that the sea, in the east, glittering? Never. A mirage. The sea's in the west, rising behind the hills that damn it up from the desert. (*A thought hits him.*) Could I break through the dam? Life this desert with water? Flood this grave and it becomes an ocean. Boats cutting through like birds – healthy air destroying the steamy vapours. And in the middle of my ocean, in a fat oasis, I will transport the Norwegian race. Our blood's nearly royal and a bit of Arab shagging will get us there. I will establish the capital around a bay on an elevated shore and I will call it Peeropolis. The old world is out of fashion. Give me your tired, your poor, your huddled masses, come to Gyntiana, my new found land. (*He leaps up.*) Find the finance and it's done. Misers shall throw their money at me. Money from east to west, all for a kingdom – my kingdom – half my kingdom for a horse.

(*The horse whinnies in the gully.*)

A horse. Clothes. Jewels. Swords. (*He goes nearer.*) This

cannot be. It is. It is real. I know faith can move mountains, but a horse? Nonsense. But here is a horse, and here's the works. (*He puts on the clothes and looks down over himself.*) Sir Peter, a Turk from tip to toe. Who knows what can happen in this life? (*He gallops into the desert.*)

SCENE 6

The tent of an Arab chief, solitary, in an oasis. In Eastern dress, PEER GYNT *reclines on cushions. He drinks coffee and smokes a long pipe.* ANITRA *and a flock of girls dance and sing before him.*

CHORUS: Sound flute, sound drum,
　　　The prophet has come.
　　　The prophet has come.
　　　Never failing Master,
　　　All knowing one,
　　　Sound flute, sound drum,
　　　The prophet has come.
ANITRA: Bend your knee,
　　　Lower head,
　　　Milk, his steed,
　　　Like Paradise,
　　　Streams. Stars, his eyes,
　　　Gently, look, look,
　　　At light's starlight.
　　　Gold and pearl
　　　Be his breast.
　　　Son of the earth,
　　　Proclaim yourself,
　　　Kaba, Kaba, empty.
PEER GYNT: The dear children I stumbled upon have declared the Prophet has come. I won't deceive them. There is a difference between lying and prophetizing. And I can back out of it at any time. It's quite a private matter. Go as I

came, the horse is ready. Really, I am master of the
situation.

ANITRA: (*Approaches the entrance*) Prophet, Master?

PEER GYNT: What does my slave girl want?

ANITRA: Outside the tent the sons of the plain await. They beg
to behold thy countenance.

PEER GYNT: Stop. Line them up at a distance and tell them I
can hear prayer at long range. Add that men are not
permitted in here. My child, avoid all men. Despicable
creatures. You cannot imagine, Anitra, how they've
cheated – I mean sinned against me. Well, that's that.
Dance for me, Anitra. The Prophet wishes to be relieved
from disturbing memories. (PEER GYNT's *eyes follow*
ANITRA *as she dances*.) A tasty piece of meat, that girlie.
What could she not get up to? Her feet aren't exactly clean,
nor her hands, especially one. But what harm? It's part of
the attraction. Anitra, listen to me.
(ANITRA *approaches*.)

PEER GYNT: You tempt me, child. You move the Prophet.
Believe me, I can prove it. I will make you a houri in
Paradise.

ANITRA: Impossible, Master. Do you think I joke? I'm serious.
I have no soul.

PEER GYNT: That you can get.

ANITRA: How, Lord?

PEER GYNT: Leave that to me. I shall provide your instruction.
Let me measure the size of your brain. I knew it, you have
room enough. You will never be profound, but you won't
be disgraced.

ANITRA: The Prophet is good –

PEER GYNT: Why do you hesitate? Speak up.

ANITRA: I did rather wish –

PEER GYNT: Speak, speak.

ANITRA: The soul, I don't care about. Give me instead –

PEER GYNT: What?

ANITRA: (*Points to his turban*) That beautiful opal.
(*Enchanted, he hands her the jewel.*)

PEER GYNT: Anitra, true daughter of Eve. I am drawn by a
magnet, for I am a man and as one well-known author has
said, woman draws us, internally, towards her. (PEER
dances and sings as night falls.)

PEER GYNT: My keys locked up Paradise
And I set out for sea,
The north breeze told the women,
I heard them mourn for me.

Anitra, Anitra, I eat
And drink your name,
Cheese and meat and sweets
And sweet is your wine.

ANITRA: My Lord, your lips ooze the honey of jest.

PEER GYNT: Little girl, don't judge great men by their cover.
I'm quite jolly, especially *à deux*. In my position I must
wear a severe mask, daily duties demand it. My concerns
make me act the stern Prophet, but that's only for form's
sake. Away with masks. In *tête-à-tête*, I am Peer, that's who
I really am. Now, chase away the Prophet. It's me, all me,
you have.
(*He sits down under a tree and pulls her towards him.* ANITRA
lies down by his feet.)

ANITRA: Your words are like sweet songs, but I understand
little. Lord, answer me, can your daughter catch a soul by
listening?

PEER GYNT: The soul isn't everything. It is the heart that
counts.

ANITRA: When you speak, Lord, I see the glint of opals.

PEER GYNT: My child, this world is stuffed with people
crammed with souls who can barely understand anything. I
knew one like that, a veritable pearl, he lost direction and
lost all. Do you know what it is to live?

ANITRA: Teach me.

PEER GYNT: Time is a river, glide down it, dry-footed. Be completely, be absolutely one's self. I want to possess your desires. In my empire of love; I shall rule by force. Gold and precious gems obsess you. So shall I. Should we part, life is over, well yours is, you should note that. I wish to fill every inch of you with me. Your hair at midnight shall hang like the Gardens of Babylon and I shall come for my regal pleasure. So it's just as well your brain is empty. When you've a soul, you contemplate yourself. Leave the soul business to me and the rest can carry on.

(ANITRA *snores*.)

PEER GYNT: Ah, she sleeps. Has not a word hit home? Still it proves my power that as I flow with loving words, she drifts into dreams. Sleep, Anitra, dream of Peer. Asleep, you place the crown on the brow of your Emperor.

SCENE 7

A caravan-road. The oasis is far behind in the distance. On his white horse, PEER GYNT *rides through the desert. In front of him, he has* ANITRA *in the saddle.*

ANITRA: Let me be. I'll bite.

PEER GYNT: You little vixen.

ANITRA: What do you want?

PEER GYNT: Want? To play. Dovy and hawky. Want to kidnap you. Play tricks.

ANITRA: You should be ashamed. Old Prophet.

PEER GYNT: Nonsense, little goosie. Prophet isn't old. Do you think this points to old age?

ANITRA: Let go. I want to go home.

PEER GYNT: Don't hover too long in one place, child. What one gains in experience, one loses in elevation, particularly if one comes as a Prophet. Appear out of air and leave like a vision.

ANITRA: Yes, but are you a Prophet?

PEER GYNT: I am your Emperor. (*He tries to kiss her.*) Oh, look how the little birdie flaps her wings.

ANITRA: Give me the ring off your finger.

PEER GYNT: Sweet Anitra, take it, take all the rubbish.

ANITRA: Your words sound like sweet songs.

PEER GYNT: But I'm young, Anitra, remember. Don't mind my antics. Laughter's for young men. When your lover is a prankster, he is therefore young, and you would understand this, my lily, if you weren't thick as a plank.

ANITRA: You are young, yes. Have you more rings?

PEER GYNT: Grab. I can leap like a deer. If there were vine leaves here, I would garland myself. Swear to God, I'm young. (*He dances and sings.*)

I am a happy little cock,
Pecking at my little hen,
Hey, hop, let me in,
I am a happy little cock.

ANITRA: Prophet, you perspire. You might melt away. Give me that heavy weight dangling from your belt.

PEER GYNT: How tender, how considerate. Carry the purse forever. Hearts in love are content without gold. (*He dances and sings again.*)

Young Peer Gynt is a zany little git
And he doesn't know where he stands,
He sleeps on his feet and walks on his hands,
That Peer Gynt who's a zany little git.

ANITRA: I am delighted that the Prophet can dance.

PEER GYNT: To hell with the Prophet. Let's swap clothes. Come on. Get them off.

ANITRA: Your dress would be too long, your corset too large, your stockings too tight.

PEER GYNT: Right. (*He kneels.*) Then punish me. Make me

suffer. Sharply, sweetly. Hearts that love, love to suffer.
Listen, when we come home to my castle –
ANITRA: In Paradise. Is it far to ride?
PEER GYNT: A thousand miles.
ANITRA: Too far.
PEER GYNT: That soul I promised you, it's there.
ANITRA: Thank you, I can manage without a soul. But you
asked to suffer.
(PEER *gets up.*)
PEER GYNT: Yes, destruction, death, violent death, but a short
one, two days, three.
ANITRA: Anitra obeys the Prophet. Farewell.
(ANITRA *gives him a sharp rap on the knuckles. She sets off in
a tearing gallop back through the desert.* PEER *stands still for a
long time, thunder-struck.*)
PEER GYNT: The witch. She was within a hair's breadth of
turning my head. Devil take me if I understand what made
me so giddy and drunk. Well, it's over. Being a Prophet's a
bastard of a job. The work lets you wander lonely as a
cloud. Everyone looking up to the Prophet, but then if you
behave like a sane man, you're dead! (*He bursts out
laughing.*) Dancing and singing and end up like a right
cock, letting yourself be plucked. Plucked yes, I've been
badly plucked. Damn it, I've a bit put aside. Something in
America, something in my pocket. I am still master of the
situation. So it's on to something new. A different
direction, a better way forward. Some purpose worth the
time and money. What if I wrote up my life as a book of
guidance and example? Or wait a minute, I'm master of my
time. I've travelled. I'm an expert – I will map the destiny
of the human race. Kingdoms founded, kingdoms
perished, small beginnings, great conclusions – I'll skim the
cream of history. All right, I'm not what would be classed a
scholar and history's inner workings are hard, but let it be,
when you start off wrongly, who knows where you might

end up – A goal has been set, I feel uplifted, I'll head for it with flint and steel. (*He is quietly moved.*) Break the ties to home and friends. Bid goodnight to love's happiness. All to find the mystery of truth. (*He dries a tear from his eye.*) Is that not a true Man of Reason? I feel happy beyond words. Now, I know the answer. Peer Gynt, Emperor of humanity.

SCENE 8

A summer's day. The far north. A hut deep in the forest, with reindeer antlers over the door. A flock of goats by the wall of the house. A middle-aged woman, SOLVEIG, *fair and beautiful, spins in the open sun. She looks down the road and sings.*

WOMAN: Winter will pass while spring does wait,
         And summer waits for New Year.
         It will come and you will come, wain,
         Promise made is promise kept, hear.

         Hear me, God, give you strength to move,
         Through the earth to his joyous door.
         I'll wait for you here, my one love,
         Or in heaven we'll pace the floor.

SCENE 9

Near the village of Gizeh. The Great Sphinx carved out of the cliff. Far away Cairo's towers and minarets. PEER GYNT *arrives.*

PEER GYNT: Egypt. Gyntian Egypt. Here's a good place to start my speculations. What does this remind me of? North or south, I've met it. Is it lion or woman? (*He goes nearer.*) Do you still know riddles? (*He calls out to the Sphinx.*) Who are you?

(*A voice comes from behind Sphinx.*)

VOICE: *Ach Sphinx, wer bist du?*

PEER GYNT: The echo speaks German. Remarkable!

VOICE: *Wer bist du?*

PEER GYNT: Speaks it perfectly. Now that's a new observation, and it's mine. (*He writes in the notebook.*) Echo in German, dialect Berlin.

(BEGRIFFENFELDT *comes from behind the Sphinx.*)

BEGRIFFENFELDT: A human.

PEER GYNT: Oh. (*He writes again.*) Shortly arrived at different conclusion.

(BEGRIFFENFELDT *moves with all kinds of agitated gestures.*)

BEGRIFFENFELDT: Dear Sir, forgive me. *Eine lebensfrage –* What brings you here today exactly?

PEER GYNT: A visit. Looking up an old friend.

BEGRIFFENFELDT: What? The Sphinx?

(PEER GYNT *nods.*)

PEER GYNT: I knew him in the old days.

BEGRIFFENFELDT: Extraordinary. I've had such a night. My forehead's a machine, it is near to bursting. You know him, sir? Speak. Tell. What is he? Tell.

PEER GYNT: Himself. He is himself!

(BEGRIFFENFELDT *leaps up.*)

BEGRIFFENFELDT: *Ja.* The riddle of life flashed before my eyes like lightning – it is certain that he is himself?

PEER GYNT: Well, so he says.

BEGRIFFENFELDT: Himself. It is the time for revolution. (*He takes off his hat.*) Name, dear sir, yours?

PEER GYNT: I was christened Peer Gynt. (*He speaks with quiet admiration.*)

BEGRIFFENFELDT: Peer Gynt. An allegory. To be expected. Peer Gynt. It means the unknown. The Messiah, and I was foretold of his advent.

PEER GYNT: Really? Have you come to meet –

BEGRIFFENFELDT: Peer Gynt. Profound. Strange. Every word, profound instruction. What are you?

PEER GYNT: (*Modestly*) I have tried always to be myself. Besides, here's my passport.

(BEGRIFFENFELDT *grabs him by the wrists.*)

BEGRIFFENFELDT: Again the mysterious subtext. To Cairo. The Emperor of Signs. The Emperor of Tongues.

PEER GYNT: Emperor?

BEGRIFFENFELDT: Come.

PEER GYNT: Have I really been heard of?

(BEGRIFFENFELDT *pulls* PEER *along.*)

BEGRIFFENFELDT: The Emperor of Signs. The Emperor of Tongues. The Messiah of the Self.

SCENE 10

Cairo. A large courtyard with high brick walls and buildings around. Barred windows and iron cages. Three guards in the yard, a fourth arriving.

FOURTH: Shafmann, where's the Director?

GUARD: He drove out this morning well before daybreak.

SECOND: Something's annoying him, because of last night –

THIRD: Ssh. He's at the door.

(BEGRIFFENFELDT *leads* PEER GYNT *in, locks the gate and puts the key in his pocket.* PEER *talks to himself.*)

PEER GYNT: This is a very gifted man. Everything he says is quite beyond me. (*He looks around.*) So this is the scholars' common room?

BEGRIFFENFELDT: Here you will find them all. The circle of seventy-two experts of signs and tongues, recently enlarged to one hundred and thirty. (*He calls out to the guards.*) You four, into the cages, at once.

GUARDS: Us?

BEGRIFFENFELDT: Who else? Go, go. The world spins and we

spin with it. (*He forces them into a cage.*) He came this
morning, the great Peer. Guess the rest, I'll say no more.
(*He locks the cage and throws the key into the well.*)

PEER GYNT: My good doctor, good director –

BEGRIFFENFELDT: Neither, neither – that was before. Mr Peer,
can you keep a secret?

(PEER *is increasingly uneasy.*)

PEER GYNT: What is it?

BEGRIFFENFELDT: Promise you won't faint.

PEER GYNT: I'll try.

(*He pulls* PEER *into a corner and whispers.*)

BEGRIFFENFELDT: Pure reason passed away this evening at 11
o'clock.

PEER GYNT: God help us all.

BEGRIFFENFELDT: Yes, terribly sad. And in my position doubly
disturbing. This institution, until quite recently, was
regarded as a mad house.

PEER GYNT: Mad house?

BEGRIFFENFELDT: Not now, you understand.

(PEER *grows white-faced and quiet.*)

PEER GYNT: Now I know this place. And the man is mad. And
nobody knows it.

(PEER *draws back, followed by* BEGRIFFENFELDT.)

BEGRIFFENFELDT: Anyway, I hope you do understand.

PEER GYNT: Excuse me a moment.

BEGRIFFENFELDT: When I say he's dead – pure reason –

PEER GYNT: How do I get out of here in safety?

BEGRIFFENFELDT: He left himself and jumped out of his skin.
A chop across the neck, and whoops, where's my skin?

PEER GYNT: Mad, stark, staring mad.

BEGRIFFENFELDT: Clear as daylight, have to come out. Reason
took leave of himself and the consequence shall be a total
revolution on land and on sea where those who were
deemed mad before 11 o'clock this evening are now quite
normal, conforming with sanity in its new manifestation,

with the further consequence that at the aforementioned time, those who were formally decreed sane are now raving lunatics.

PEER GYNT: You mention time, my time is precious –

BEGRIFFENFELDT: Your time? Of course, you must advance. (*He opens a door and calls out.*) Come forward. The new age is announced. Sanity is dead. Long live Peer Gynt. (*The lunatics come out into the yard.*)

PEER GYNT: My dear fellow –

BEGRIFFENFELDT: Good morning. Come and greet the age of freedom. Your Emperor has come.

PEER GYNT: Emperor?

BEGRIFFENFELDT: Yes, indeed.

PEER GYNT: Too great an honour, beyond –

BEGRIFFENFELDT: This is no time for false modesty.

PEER GYNT: Give me a little time, I'm not up to it. I feel quite stupid.

BEGRIFFENFELDT: A man who has deciphered the meaning of the Sphinx? Who is himself?

PEER GYNT: That's precisely the problem. In every respect I am myself. Here, however, it's more a question of being beside oneself.

BEGRIFFENFELDT: Beside? Totally wrong. Here one is absolutely, utterly and only oneself, not the tiniest particle any other self. Full steam ahead to the self. Here the self is steeped in a barrel and as the self ferments, so it closes itself like a hermit into the cell of the self and swells the wood in the well of the self. Who weeps here at another's fears? Who feels here for another's ideas? We are ourselves alone, in thought and time, ourselves alone at the very edge of the precipice, and so if we elect an Emperor to our throne, you are the right man.

PEER GYNT: I would like to be the devil.

BEGRIFFENFELDT: Don't be shy. When you are born, everything is strange. Oneself alone, there's an example. I

72

shall choose the first at random. (*He speaks to a brooding man.*) Good day, Huhu. Why are you always wearing the mask of gloom?

HUHU: How can I not when generation after generation die without a voice? (*He speaks to* PEER GYNT.) You are a stranger. Will you listen?

PEER GYNT: (*Bows*) By all means.

(HUHU *conveys his lament in the style of a certain race of tenor.*)

HUHU: There is a country in the east that is called Old Malabar.
Portuguese and Dutchmen came there from across seas so far.
The Malabars lived by their own ways and by their own laws.
But the strangers mixed the language and disaster's what we saw.
In the old days lived a people, we call them Orang-Utang.
They possessed the forest freely wherein they roamed in gangs.
They did scream till the foreigner said, your ways you must mend.
And so began the curse that is without end.
Four centuries of oppression fell upon the monkey tribe,
and you could not sing an old song unless you gave a bribe.
No more growling, no more gasping, no more screaming anymore,
it's all words we share between us, oh, grief, out it pours.
Men like me shall fight for our right to roar our heads
off in the night, in the forest, in the old songs I've led.
But do you think that they will listen to my old lament?
Now you know my sorrow surely, and why my head is bent.

(*He stops singing.*) Thank you for your sympathy. If you know a cure, will you let me know?

PEER GYNT: When you see wolves, howl with them. (*He takes up the lament.*) Dear friend, in old Morocco live the proud

73

Orang-Utang,

and they live in states of screaming of which you have just sang.

Pure and precious was their language, it was sheer Malabar.

Maybe you and all like you should go there so very far away.

HUHU: Thank you, you're very good. I'll do as you say. (*He makes an expansive gesture before exit.*) Let the east reject the singer, the west's awake with Orang-Utangs.

BEGRIFFENFELDT: Was he full of himself? I should say so. Himself alone. Himself in the power of himself. Come. I will show you another who, since last night, has no less than the last been confirmed a sane man. (*He speaks to a fellah, an Egyptian peasant, who carries a mummy on his back.*) How are things, King Apis? Your Highness?

(*The* FELLAH *turns to* PEER GYNT.)

FELLAH: Am I King Apis?

(PEER *hides behind the doctor.*)

PEER GYNT: Well now, unfortunately, I am not aquainted with the situation, but I do believe, if appearances are anything to go by –

FELLAH: You're a liar as well.

BEGRIFFENFELDT: Your Highness must report on the situation.

FELLAH: Then I will. (*He turns to* PEER GYNT.) This man I carry upon my back once answered to a name. King Apis that was is now embalmed, for he is dead, dead. Pyramids, the great Sphinx, they were the work of his hand. He made war and was praised as a god. Egypt placed him in her temples in the likeness of a bull. And I am King Apis, do you understand? You will, you will. King Apis was a hunter, one day, down from his horse, he went into a field of my grandfather to relieve himself. The field he fertilized nourished me with corn. Do you need further proof? Look, look at my horns. And I am cursed, for no one praises me by right. I am King Apis, but this country thinks me scum. What have I to do to become like the great King?

PEER GYNT: Build pyramids, carve the Sphinx, make great war.

FELLAH: I'm nobody, less than a louse, enough to do freeing my shack of rats and mice. Quick man, think of something else. Make me great and solid. Make me like the King I carry on my back.

PEER GYNT: Find a rope and hang yourself in the bosom of the earth, feel the walls of your coffin, be dead, die.

FELLAH: I will. My life for a rope. Lead me to the gallows. At the start it will be difficult, but time heals all. (*He goes away, preparing to hang himself.*)

BEGRIFFENFELDT: That was a real personality. A man with a method, Mr Peer.

PEER GYNT: Yes, yes, he was. But he's really hanging himself. God have mercy on us all. I feel sick. I'm losing control of my mind –

BEGRIFFENFELDT: A period of transition. It will pass.

PEER GYNT: Transition? Where to? Excuse me – I must go – (BEGRIFFENDFELDT *holds on to him.*)

BEGRIFFENFELDT: Are you mad?

PEER GYNT: Mad? Not yet. God help me.

(*A noise. The Minister* HUSSAIN *presses through the crowd.*)

HUSSAIN: I have been informed an Emperor arrived today. (*He speaks to* PEER GYNT.) It is you?

PEER GYNT: (*Despairing*) Yes. It seems to be so decided.

HUSSAIN: Good. Then there are some queries to be answered? (PEER *pulls at his hair.*)

PEER GYNT: Of course. The more lunatic the better.

HUSSAIN: Perhaps you will honour me with a quick dip? (*He bows deeply.*) I am a pen.

(PEER *bows even deeper.*)

PEER GYNT: And I am a piece of wrinkled, imperial paper.

HUSSAIN: Sir, to put it briefly, I am thought of as grains of sand, but I am a pen.

PEER GYNT: I too will be brief, sir. I am a sheet of paper, untouched.

HUSSAIN: My capabilities are not recognized. I am simply sprinkled like sand to dry up ink.

PEER GYNT: Once a woman pressed me in a book with a silver clasp. Being sane or mad is all the one mistake.

HUSSAIN: Imagine the frustration, being a pen with no point.

PEER GYNT: (*Jumps high*) Imagine never feeling earth beneath your reindeer hoof.

HUSSAIN: I am blunt. Let me be sharpened. I need a knife. The world will end if I am not sharpened.

BEGRIFFENFELDT: Here is a knife.

HUSSAIN: (*Grabs it*) I shall really drown in ink. How blissful to rip oneself. (*He cuts his throat.*)

(BEGRIFFENFELDT *gets out of his way.*)

BEGRIFFENFELDT: Don't spill out.

(PEER's *terror mounts.*)

PEER GYNT: Hold him –

HUSSAIN: Hold, that is the word, hold, hold the pen, put paper on the table – (*He falls.*) I am dried out. Do not forget my PS. As he lived, so did he die, a guided pen.

(PEER *grows dizzy.*)

PEER GYNT: What shall I – what am I – God, save me – I am – Whatever you like I am – Turk, sinner, troll – help me – something's burst – (PEER *screams.*) Your name – forgotten – help – Guardian of fools. (*He sinks down in a faint.*)

(BEGRIFFENFELDT *leaps beside him, a wreath of straw in his hand.*)

BEGRIFFENFELDT: See how he soars in the mud. Quite beside himself. Let his coronation take place. (*He places the wreath down on* PEER's *head, exclaiming*) The Emperor is alive. Long live the Emperor of the Self.

(*From the cage, a guard,* SCHAFMANN, *calls.*)

SCHAFMANN: *Eslebe hoch der grosse Peer.*

76

ACT FIVE

SCENE I

*A boat in the North Sea, outside the Norwegian coast. It is sunset.
The weather is stormy. A strong old man, with hair and beard the
colour of ice,* PEER GYNT *stands on the ship, half dressed as a
sailor, in a jacket and high boots. He is down at heel, his clothes
somewhat half worn. He himself is weather beaten, wearing a
harder expression. The* CAPTAIN *of the ship stands with the
Helmsman. The crew are to the front of the ship.* PEER GYNT *leans
his arms on the rail and stares towards the shore.*

PEER GYNT: Look at him, the old fella, Hallingskarcen, showing
      himself off, in the top coat, glorying in the sun this evening.
      That's the brother, Jokelen, behind him, still not shedding the
      green winter coat. Look at her, the Folgefonn, the slip of a girl,
      the virgin in white. Pure. Hi, old boys, hold your ground. Stay
      put. She's where she is, and so are you.
      (*The* CAPTAIN *calls forward to the crew.*)
CAPTAIN: Two men to the wheel – lantern fixed.
PEER GYNT: Hard wind.
CAPTAIN: Storm, tonight.
PEER GYNT: Can you catch Ronden from the sea?
CAPTAIN: Unlikely. Behind the snow.
PEER GYNT: Blaaho?
CAPTAIN: No. Up above, when there's a clearing, you can see
      Galdopeak.
PEER GYNT: Where would you find Haartrigen?
CAPTAIN: (*Pointing*) Thereabouts.
PEER GYNT: Yes, right.
CAPTAIN: You know where you are.
PEER GYNT: Leaving here, this country, I passed by these
      places. You know what they say, dregs in the glass taste on
      your mouth longer. (*He spits and stares at the coast.*) See,

where the glens cliff into a blue, and there where the
mountain valleys into black, beneath the fjord, where it's
open, there are people living there – (*He looks at the*
CAPTAIN.) In this country they keep their distance.

CAPTAIN: They respect what divides them.

PEER GYNT: Are we in by daylight?

CAPTAIN: Provided the night isn't fierce.

PEER GYNT: It's thickening in the west.

CAPTAIN: It is.

PEER GYNT: Enough. Remind me when we're settling up to
remember the crew.

CAPTAIN: That's kind of you.

PEER GYNT: Only a token. I've dug for gold, found it and lost
it. Myself and Fate weren't at one. You know what I cargo.
That's what there is. The Devil took the rest.

CAPTAIN: People at home would think that enough to make you
a man.

PEER GYNT: No family waiting for the ugly, rich man. So be it.
Spared the fussing on the quay. So remind yourself if any
man here is wanting, money means little to me.

CAPTAIN: Handsome of you. They're poor men, most of them.
Wife and a house of young ones waiting. On what they
earn, times are thin. To come home with extra money
would be a big night they won't forget.

PEER GYNT: Are they married?

CAPTAIN: Married? The whole lot, yes. The worst off is the
cook. Black hunger in that house.

PEER GYNT: Married? Someone waiting at home, have they,
who lifts the roof when they walk in? Yes?

CAPTAIN: Yes, you know the way the poor give –

PEER GYNT: When they walk in, one evening, what happens?

CAPTAIN: The wife manages to find grub that's good for once –

PEER GYNT: And the candle's blessed?

CAPTAIN: Maybe two, with a wet whistle to chase the bite in
your mouth –

PEER GYNT: And there they sit, at their ease. There's a fire
    burning. Gathered the children about them. The room's
    living. Nobody lets anybody finish. Is that how happy –
    happy – they are?
CAPTAIN: Maybe so. So it was a handsome promise you just
    made, to heavy the pocket –
PEER GYNT: Do you think I'm mad? Am I going to shell out for
    the benefit of another man's child? I sweated sore to earn
    my pounds and pence. Nobody's waiting for Peer Gynt,
    nobody's waiting for an old man.
CAPTAIN: Right, right. As you like. Your money's yours.
PEER GYNT: Right. Mine, nobody else's. Settle up when we
    drop anchor. A ticket from Panama as a cabin passenger.
    Brandy for the boys. Nothing more. If I give more,
    Captain, slap my mouth shut.
CAPTAIN: I owe you a bill, not a beating. (*He goes forward on the
    deck.*)
    (*It has grown dark. Light comes on in the cabins. The sun
    rises. Fog and thick cloud fall.*)
PEER GYNT: A pack of children running wild about the house –
    joy in your mind, as you walk the earth, they walk with
    you. Who is there to think of me? They have their
    children. They've seen the light. Well, the light will be put
    out. I'll think of something. Have them drunk to the gills
    and send them home stinking. Reeling back to wife and
    family. Curse in the mouth and bang on the table. Scare
    the shite out of all waiting. The wife opens her throat and
    clears the house. Children in her trail. Happy days be at an
    end, game be gone.
    (*The ship lurches.* PEER GYNT *stumbles and holds himself up
    with difficulty.*)
    That was a girl of a heave. You'd swear the sea was being
    paid. The north's the north when it comes to the water.
    Makes up its own mind, contrary and awkward –
LOOK OUT: Wreck to leeward.

CAPTAIN: Hard a-starboard. Get her to the wind.

MATE: Who's going down?

LOOK OUT: Three out.

PEER GYNT: Get a boat lowered. (*He goes forward.*)

CAPTAIN: Overturned before we move.

PEER GYNT: Who gives a damn? Save them. (*He speaks to the crew.*) Are you men? Save them. So your feet get wet, does the devil –

BOSUN: In this water, forget it.

PEER GYNT: They're roaring again. The wind's dropping. Come on, Cook, would you chance it? Come on, I'll pay –

COOK: Not for twenty pounds in my hand –

PEER GYNT: You shower of cowards. They have a wife and young ones at home. Are they sitting waiting –

BOSUN: Take your time, that's what counts.

LOOK OUT: She's gone.

BOSUN: You thought them married, now think them widowed. (*The storm rises.* PEER GYNT *goes alone about the deck.*)

PEER GYNT: Is there one honest man among Christians? Nights like these, Jesus is dangerous. Pick no fight with him. Me, I'm blameless: this shower go and look for bother. They say a good conscience is a good pillow. That holds on dry land but what's it count for a decent man among sailors? On the water, forget yourself. Bosun and Cook, their time might come and I'll go sharp with them down the sluice. I should think of myself more. Act the boss. I would if I were in my prime. Ah, to hell with time! There's still time enough to let them know in this town, Peer has crossed the ocean. Peer will win back the farm by fair means or foul. Peer will build it up and nobody will be allowed into the good front room. They will stand, cap in hand, in front of the gate. They will try, they will beseech – but every penny is mine. I was the one who God's whip beat into crying and it's time I did the beating. (*A strange* TRAVELLER *stands beside* PEER GYNT *and greets him like a friend.*)

TRAVELLER: Soft evening.

PEER GYNT: Soft. What? Who are you?

TRAVELLER: Travelling with you. Neither here nor there. As you'd want.

PEER GYNT: Was I not the only one?

TRAVELLER: So you thought. That's over.

PEER GYNT: Strange enough, tonight's the first time I've seen you –

TRAVELLER: I never see daylight.

PEER GYNT: Are you not well? White as a sheet –

TRAVELLER: Thank you, no. I'm in the best of form –

PEER GYNT: Fierce storm.

TRAVELLER: Yes, aren't we blessed?

PEER GYNT: Blessed?

TRAVELLER: High as a house, this sea. It makes my mouth water. Imagine it crushing the wrecks. Imagine the corpses drifting ashore.

PEER GYNT: My Christ.

TRAVELLER: Have you ever seen a man with life torn out of him, hanging or drowning –

PEER GYNT: This is getting too –

TRAVELLER: Dead men laugh. But I don't believe their laughter. Most of them have bitten out their tongues.

PEER GYNT: Get away from me.

TRAVELLER: Say we sank in the dark –

PEER GYNT: Is it that dangerous?

TRAVELLER: I don't know. But say I swim and you sink –

PEER GYNT: Rubbish.

TRAVELLER: Perhaps. When one foot is in the grave, people soften and give –

PEER GYNT: Oh, money –

TRAVELLER: No, give me your corpse, for the sake of my research, you understand.

PEER GYNT: Go away from me.

TRAVELLER: But think, my dear. I will open you up by light of day and locate the centre of your dreams.

PEER GYNT: Get thee behind me.

TRAVELLER: My dear, a drowned body –

PEER GYNT: Isn't there enough in the sea and the storm to warn us of the end, and you will it on sooner.

TRAVELLER: You are not in the mood for making bargains. Still, time changes all things. When you're sinking, shall we meet then? Maybe earlier. Perhaps you will be in better humour then. (*Goes into the cabin.*)

PEER GYNT: Damn your research. Damn your science. Atheist. (*The* BOSUN *walks past.*)

PEER GYNT: Friend, that passenger, what kind of lunatic –

BOSUN: Only you travel with us.

PEER GYNT: No others? What is happening?

(*A* SEAMAN *walks past.*)

PEER GYNT: Who went in through the cabin door?

SEAMAN: The ship's dog, sir. (*He walks by.*)

LOOK OUT: (*Shouts*) Land ahead.

PEER GYNT: My cases. My luggage. All goods on deck.

BOSUN: We have other things to bother us.

PEER GYNT: I was only joking, Captain. Of course I'll help the Cook.

CAPTAIN: The jib's a goner.

MATE: The foresail's down.

BOSUN: Rocks.

CAPTAIN: She's breaking up.

(*The ship runs aground. Noise and confusion.*)

SCENE 2

Near land. Rocks and spray. The ship goes down. Through fog, a dinghy with two men. The sea fills it. It overturns. A cry. Quietness. Soon the upturned keel appears. PEER GYNT *surfaces.*

PEER GYNT: Help me. Help. I'm dying. Lord Jesus, be my

Saviour, are you, say you are. (*He clings to the keel.*)
(*The* COOK *surfaces on the other side.*)

COOK: Lord God, for the sake of my youngsters, have mercy on me. Let me reach land. (*He holds on to the keel.*)

PEER GYNT: Let go.

COOK: Let go.

PEER GYNT: I'll hit –

COOK: I'll hit back.

PEER GYNT: Do you want your head kicked in? Let go. This won't carry two.

COOK: I know. Give way.

PEER GYNT: Give way yourself.

COOK: Yes?
(*They fight. The* COOK *hurts his hand, and clings fast with the other.*)

PEER GYNT: Get that hand away.

COOK: Please, spare me. Think of my young ones at home.

PEER GYNT: I need life more than you do, I have no children.

COOK: Let go. You've lived. I'm young.

PEER GYNT: Sink, damn you. You're growing heavy.

COOK: Mercy. In God's name, give way. Who'll mourn you? Who'll miss you? (*He screams and lets go.*) I'm drowning.

PEER GYNT: (*Grabbing him*) I'm holding you by the scruff of the neck. Say the Our Father.

COOK: Can't remember – world's dark –

PEER GYNT: Say quick –

COOK: Give us this day –

PEER GYNT: Leave that out, what you need you'll get, Cook.

COOK: Give us this day –

PEER GYNT: Same tune. You were once a Cook.
(*The grip slips.*)

COOK: Give us this day our – (*He goes under.*)

PEER GYNT: Amen, son. You were what you were to the end.
(*He swings himself on to the keel.*)
(*The strange* TRAVELLER *grabs hold of the boat.*)

83

TRAVELLER: Good morning.

PEER GYNT: What?

TRAVELLER: I heard shouting. How nice to find you. May I inquire after your corpse?

PEER GYNT: Shut your mouth.

TRAVELLER: As you wish.

(*Silence.*)

PEER GYNT: What is it now?

TRAVELLER: I am quiet.

PEER GYNT: The devil's tactic. What are you doing?

TRAVELLER: Waiting.

(PEER GYNT *tears his head.*)

PEER GYNT: I'm going mad. What are you?

TRAVELLER: Friendly.

PEER GYNT: Speak.

TRAVELLER: What do you think? Do you know any like me?

PEER GYNT: I know the devil –

TRAVELLER: (*Quietly*) Does he light the lantern when the night of life darkens the road of fear?

PEER GYNT: So are you a messenger of light?

TRAVELLER: Friend, even once in a blue moon have you felt the depth, the weight of fear?

PEER GYNT: There's fear when there's danger, but you twist your words –

TRAVELLER: Yes, have you even once in your life felt the triumph that is won through fear?

PEER GYNT: (*Looking at him*) If you came to show me the way, why wasn't it before now? The sea's going to swallow us –

TRAVELLER: Would the triumph have been easier by your fireside, safe and sound?

PEER GYNT: You're mocking me. Scarecrow, get out of my sight. I don't want to die. I'll reach land.

TRAVELLER: Then be brave. You can't die in the middle of Act Five. (*Glides away.*)

PEER GYNT: You came to say that. You preaching prig.

A churchyard, high up in the mountains. A funeral. The PRIEST
and congregation. PEER GYNT *walks by. He stands at the gate. The*
PRIEST *speaks at the graveside.*

PRIEST: This man was not rich, nor was he wise. Meek,
unmanly, barely master in his own house. He moved here
as a lad, and as you will all remember, never took the right
hand out of his pocket. That marked him out and the
shyness. A quiet being, a lifelong stranger, but you all
know that his one hand had only four fingers. I can
remember, long ago, it was a time of war. Young lads
answered the call, one by one. When his turn came, he
entered the recruiting office pale, gasping for words,
speechless. His right hand covered in a cloth – What is
that? The Captain ordered. His cheeks burned, his tongue
failed, he mumbled something about a scythe. The Captain
turned the boy to stone. He stood up, his lip curled and he
roared. Go. He went. He ran. To the mountains. His
home. Six months later here he was with mother, wife and
child. He did quite well on his small patch of land. Worked
terribly hard, and hid his hand. Then there was the flood.
Flattened him. He rose up and built again. No more floods
to fear. But he forgot about the glacier. Flattened him. All
over again. He tried once more and raised anew his humble
house. God blessed his union with three sons. Three fine
lads. To get to school their path was perilous. But they
made into fine men through their father's toil. Men. Could
he not, the father, expect some return? They have gone to
the New World and prospered there, forgetting their old
Norwegian father and those days spent plunging through
the gullies, so steep and narrow. He was a short-sighted
man. He saw nothing beyond his nose. Lofty words, high
ideals – faith, force and fatherland, not for him. Meek and

modest. Did he break his country's laws? Yes, all right.
But one thing transcends all laws. Yes, to church and state,
he was a rotten stick. But high up there, in the narrow
circle of Kith and Kin, he was great, because he was
himself. Rest you, silent warrior, who fought and fell in the
small farmer's war. May he stand whole, before his God.
(PRIEST *and congregation disperse and exit.* PEER GYNT *stays
alone behind them.*)

PEER GYNT: What a piece of work is Christian man. Be
yourself. So uplifting. (*He looks into the grave.*) I approve
this Christian custom of judging the dead gently – the same
may be passed on me in the grave, like this man. But not
yet, not just yet. Still the Church is a true comfort, those
reassuring voices: as you sow, so do you reap. Be yourself.
Care about you and yours in all things great and small.
Should luck desert you, then pride yourself you led life by
the rules. Old Peer Gynt goes on his way. As he is, as he
was. Poor, but honest.

SCENE 4

*Hill. A river dried up. In the distance a large farm. An auction. A
large crowd, making noise, drinking.* PEER GYNT *sits on gravel by a
milestone.*

MAN IN BLACK: It's all for nothing.
(*He sees* PEER GYNT.)
Strangers here too? God bless you, friend.

PEER GYNT: There's plenty of life here. Is it a wedding blessing
or a birth?

MAN IN BLACK: It's more a coming home, so eat your fill. The
bride's being eaten. By worms.

PEER GYNT: Are the worms fighting over rags and ribbons?

MAN IN BLACK: So the song ends.

PEER GYNT: So all songs end. Old ones. I knew them as a boy.

86

(*A* YOUTH *enters with a ladle.*)

FIRST YOUTH: Look at this beauty I've brought. Peer Gynt casts his silver buttons in it.

SECOND YOUTH: Look at this, I gave a bob for the moneybox.

PEER GYNT: Peer Gynt? Who was he?

MAN IN BLACK: He was a man related by marriage to Death and Aslak the Smith.

MAN IN GREY: You forget me. Are you mixed up, or drunk?

MAN IN BLACK: In Hagstead there was a storehouse and it had a door.

MAN IN GREY: That's true, but you were never choosy.

MAN IN BLACK: Maybe she won't cheat on Death –

MAN IN GREY: Come on, brother. A drink for the sake of kindred.

MAN IN BLACK: To hell with kindred. You're drunk –

MAN IN GREY: Rubbish. Even if the connection is hard to trace, we've all Peer Gynt's blood inside us.

(*They wander off.*)

PEER GYNT: (*Softly*) So here one meets old friends.

FIRST YOUTH: Aslak, if you get pissed again, your mother will kill you.

PEER GYNT: The more you dig, the deeper you get.

FIRST YOUTH: (*Holding a reindeer skull*) Peer Gynt raced this bucko over the Gjeudin mountain.

PEER GYNT: So they say.

FIRST YOUTH: Aslak, do you know this hammer? You hit the Devil with it.

SECOND YOUTH: Mods, do you see the invisible cloak? Peer Gynt and Ingrid wore it flying through the air.

PEER GYNT: Brandy, lads. I'm an old man. I want to auction some scrap and rubbish.

FIRST YOUTH: What have you to sell?

PEER GYNT: A palace. In the mountain. Well built.

FIRST YOUTH: A button's the bid.

PEER GYNT: Up it to a drink. Less would be a sin.

FIRST YOUTH: This old boy's good crack.

(*They flock around him.*)

PEER GYNT: My magic horse, who will bid?

FIRST YOUTH: Where does he graze?

PEER GYNT: The west, boys, where the sun sets. This horse can fly as fast as Peer Gynt can lie.

VOICES: What else have you?

PEER GYNT: Gold and glitter, bought from shipwreck, sold at a loss.

FIRST YOUTH: Keep going.

PEER GYNT: I have a dream about a prayer book. Have that for a hook in the eye.

FIRST YOUTH: To the devil with dreams.

PEER GYNT: My empire. I'll throw it to you. Squabble over it.

FIRST YOUTH: Does the crown go with it?

PEER GYNT: Of the finest straw. First to fit it has it. More, more. The prophet's beard. He has it who can point me to the sign that shows the road.

(*A PARISH SHERIFF enters.*)

SHERIFF: From the way you're behaving, my man, your road leads to prison.

(*Peer's hat is in his hands.*)

PEER GYNT: Likely. Tell me though, who was Peer Gynt?

SHERIFF: Nonsense –

PEER GYNT: Please, I beg you –

SHERIFF: A rotten storyteller.

PEER GYNT: Storyteller?

SHERIFF: Every story he made out he had done the mighty deed. Excuse me, friend, I've other business –

PEER GYNT: Where is he now, this remarkable man?

SHERIFF: Across the ocean. Did there as we all expected. He was hanged many years ago.

PEER GYNT: Hanged? Well, well. The late Peer Gynt stayed himself to the end. Farewell, and many thanks. (*He goes, but stops.*) Strong boys and lovely girls, would you like a story for reward?

CROWD: Do you know any?

PEER GYNT: What's to stop me? (*He comes nearer, with a strange look on his face.*) In San Francisco I dug for gold, the whole town was a clown's paradise. One scraped the violin with his toes, the second danced on his knees. I've heard a third wrote poetry while a drill moved through his skull. And into this company of clowns the Devil made his entrance, looking to make his fortune, like many before him. He had a skill, and it was this – he could squeal like a pig in a most deceptive manner. His manner was a mighty draw but no one knew him. He'd fill the house, raise the nerves, and appear in a swirling cape. Now, under this cape – and nobody knew – he'd hidden a real pig. The performance starts, the devil nips and the pig starts its song. It was a fantasy, you see, on the theme of our existence as pigs, slaved and freed. At the end – a squeal from the pig as if the butcher's knife had struck, after which the artist bowed with respect and left the stage. Critics chewed it over and spat it out. Good and bad, they declared, voice a little too thin, the cry of death too mannered. On one point they agreed. As a piece of playing it was completely over the top. What could he expect, the Devil? He was stupid, for he gave his audience what they didn't want.

(*An uneasy silence falls on the crowd. They disperse.*)

SCENE 5

It is the eve of Whitsun. A forest.

PEER GYNT: Idiot, old fool. You're no Emperor, you're an onion, and I shall peel you, Peer my love. (*He takes an onion and peels off layer after layer.*) The outer layer's pretty ragged, that's the man clinging to the wreck. Here's the traveller poor and thin, but still a faint taste of Peer Gynt. Inside here's the man digging for gold – no juice, had it ever? The one beyond looks like a crown. Thank you, we'll dispose of that quickly. (*He peels several in one go.*) Here's a right handful, doesn't the centre appear soon? (*He peels the whole onion.*) No, it damn well doesn't. Into the inner and it's only layers, smaller and smaller. Isn't nature a right wit? (*He throws it all away.*)

SOLVEIG: (*Sings*) It is the feast of tongued fire
    That we call Pentecost.
    Dear boy, are you heavy cast,
    Are you near, or are you far?
    Take your time, take precious time,
    Promise kept, promise mine.

(PEER GYNT *rises. He is deathly pale.*)

PEER GYNT: One remembered – and one forgot. One went – and one stayed. The truth. And there is no redemption. Fear. Here was my empire. (*He runs through the forest.*)

SCENE 6

Night. Mist. PEER GYNT *on the run.*

PEER GYNT: Is that the voice of children weeping, or is it a song?

THREADBALLS: We are thoughts you should have thought,
    shoes for feet you never bought.

(PEER GYNT *goes around them.*)

PEER GYNT: One life I gave, and it was crippled and dirty, unforgiving.

THREADBALLS: Waves of voice that storm and soar?
    No, we're dust to tramp on floors.

PEER GYNT: Stop pestering your daddy.

(*Withered leaves fly in the wind.*)

LEAVES: Did you call to create us?

Now, the worm dates us
Where's the fruit, the garland,
Dropped from your lazy hand?

PEER GYNT: No cause for weeping. Lie down and manure the
ground.

(*Sounds speak through the air.*)

AIR: We are words went unspoken,
Songs to feed your heart,
Lying, waiting in that dark den,
Poison through your body darts.

PEER GYNT: Poison you instead, did I have time for rhyming
twaddle?

(*Dewdrops sprinkle from branches.*)

DEWDROPS: We are tears that were not spilt
To wash the wound's frozen pelt.
Now the wound will wear forever,
For our power, our power is over.

PEER GYNT: Thank you, I cried in the mountain kingdom and
got a kick in the arse for it.

(*Broken straws float in the wind.*)

BROKEN STRAWS: Do you doubt your deeds undone?
Straws you broke to leave in strands.
When the Day of Judgement comes,
We shall sing like crying birds.

(ÅSE *appears.*)

ÅSE: The old boy runs home to his mother.
As you walk the earth, they walk with you.
Look where I landed, son lying in snow.
I was in your hands, you let me go.
Where's the rejoicing?
Where's the palace?
The devil's heard you, my power is over.

(ÅSE *disappears.*)

PEER GYNT: Time for a poor fool to run. The devil's sins would
kill you, and my own are heavy enough.

The BUTTONMOULDER, *with a toolbox and a large casting ladle, comes from a sideroad.*

BUTTONMOULDER: How are you, old man? You're in a hurry. Where are you going?

PEER GYNT: To a corphouse.

BUTTONMOULDER: I've bad eyes. Isn't your name Peer?

PEER GYNT: Peer Gynt, they say.

BUTTONMOULDER: Isn't that lucky? It is the selfsame Peer Gynt I've to fetch tonight.

PEER GYNT: What do you want?

BUTTONMOULDER: Here, you can see. I am a buttonmoulder, and you're for my ladle.

PEER GYNT: What for?

BUTTONMOULDER: To melt you down.

PEER GYNT: Melt?

BUTTONMOULDER: The Master's orders. I have to fetch your soul now.

PEER GYNT: Not without warning.

BUTTONMOULDER: Do you not know about birth and death? No one tells the guest of honour.

PEER GYNT: You are –

BUTTONMOULDER: You heard. A buttonmoulder.

PEER GYNT: I understand. So Peer, this is your end. But my good man, you're cheating a little. I deserve softer handling. I'm not as bad as you believed. In this life I've done considerable good. At worst, I might be called a fool, but definitely not a bad sinner.

BUTTONMOULDER: That's the problem. You're not a sinner of some importance. That's why you'll escape purgatory and end up like the rest in the melting pot.

PEER GYNT: Get thee behind me, Satan.

BUTTONMOULDER: Are you so vulgar as to imagine I travel

around on a cloven hoof? A great mistake, friend. We're both busy men. To save time I will take you to the heart of the matter. Nowadays the real sinners are few and far between. To sin requires strength and weight.

PEER GYNT: True, true word. Go at it like a man berserk.

BUTTONMOULDER: But you, sir, took sin lightly.

PEER GYNT: I wasn't afraid to get my hands dirtied.

BUTTONMOULDER: We agree.

PEER GYNT: So may I go as I came?

BUTTONMOULDER: No, friend, you'll be melted down.

PEER GYNT: Has some new device been invented while I was away?

BUTTONMOULDER: Old as the serpent in the Garden of Eden. Waste not, want not. Use every item. You were to be a shining button on the world's waistcoat, but the loop cracked. So it's in with the rejects and gather you with the mob.

PEER GYNT: Never. I'll fight tooth and claw. Anything but that.

BUTTONMOULDER: Be sensible. You're not delicate enough for heaven.

PEER GYNT: I'm a modest man. I don't look that high. But I won't give up a bit of self. Judge me by the book, the old-fashioned way. Foster me out to the devil, say for a hundred years. That I could endure moral suffering. Sit back, wait and hope for redemption. But! This – ladle-melting – business, ceasing to be Peer Gynt, sucked into some bystander's body, that sends my soul spinning.

BUTTONMOULDER: My good Peer, so much fuss over nothing. Never before have you been yourself. What does it matter if you are exterminated?

PEER GYNT: Don't make me laugh. You say Peer Gynt has perhaps been someone else? Buttonmoulder, you're blind. Look out my inner being. Peer is Peer, nothing more.

BUTTONMOULDER: Not so. I have my orders. Look at what's written. You must claim Peer Gynt. He has gone against the purpose of his life. Shoddy goods, into the ladle with him. I have it in writing.

PEER GYNT: No, wouldn't it be nice if tomorrow showed
  somebody else was intended?
BUTTONMOULDER: I have it in writing.
PEER GYNT: Give me a chance.
BUTTONMOULDER: To do what?
PEER GYNT: Prove I was myself all my life.
BUTTONMOULDER: Prove? With what?
PEER GYNT: Witnesses, references.
BUTTONMOULDER: It won't hold much sway with the Master.
PEER GYNT: Let me face my sorrows as they're flung at me.
  Give me a loan of myself. I will be back here again. You're
  only born with one single self. You'd like to hold on to the
  one created for you.
BUTTONMOULDER: All right. Agreed. But remember, we meet
  at the next crossroads.
  (PEER GYNT *runs.*)

SCENE 8

Further along the heath. PEER GYNT *is at full speed.*

PEER GYNT: A witness, where do I find a witness? Why should
  any man have to prove what's his by rights?
  (*An* OLD MAN *with a staff in his hand and a bag on his back
  trudges in front of him.*)
OLD MAN: (*Stops*) Kind man, have you a shilling for an old boy
  with no roof over his head?
PEER GYNT: Forgive me, I've no change –
OLD MAN: Prince Peer, so we should meet –
PEER GYNT: Who are you?
OLD MAN: Do you not remember the old man in the mountain?
PEER GYNT: You are not –
OLD MAN: King. The King of the Mountains.
PEER GYNT: The Mountain King, are you – Answer.
OLD MAN: I've come down in the world.

PEER GYNT: Such a witness doesn't grow on the trees.

OLD MAN: The Prince has grown old too, since the last meeting.

PEER GYNT: Well, father, time wears us all. Forget about private business, and no fights please. Look, I've got myself into a spot of trouble. I need a character reference. You'd be the man to help me out. I can see my way to a small tip.

OLD MAN: Can I be of use to the Prince?

PEER GYNT: Do you remember when I signed up as a suitor in the Mountain Kingdom? You were going to hold me down, slice my eye and transform me from Peer Gynt into a troll. I stood my ground. I renounced love and power and honour, just to be myself. You must swear that in court.

OLD MAN: No. No. Can't.

PEER GYNT: What are you saying?

OLD MAN: Do you want me to lie? Don't you remember, you wore the tail, you drank the brew –

PEER GYNT: You tempted me, you seduced me, but I didn't fall and that's how you know the mark of your man. That's what counts in the end.

OLD MAN: But the end was quite the reverse, Peer.

PEER GYNT: Nonsense.

OLD MAN: When you left my Kingdom, you took special note of my motto.

PEER GYNT: Which?

OLD MAN: To your own self be yourself alone.

PEER GYNT: Alone?

OLD MAN: And night and day so you've lived since then.

PEER GYNT: Me? Peer Gynt?

(*The* OLD MAN *weeps.*)

OLD MAN: No gratitude, not a word of thanks.

PEER GYNT: Me? A mountain troll? Rubbish, nonsense.

(*The* OLD MAN *pulls out a bundle of newspapers.*)

OLD MAN: It's in all the papers.

PEER GYNT: I am a mountain troll?

OLD MAN: Yes, that matter is clear.

PEER GYNT: So I may as well have stayed put where I was? Peer
    Gynt, a troll. Nonsense. Here's a shilling to buy tobacco.
OLD MAN: No, kind Prince Peer.
PEER GYNT: Let go. You are mad. You're a child again. Find a
    hospital.
OLD MAN: That's all I'm looking for. But we've neither poor
    box nor public charity, in the Mountain Kingdom.
PEER GYNT: True. Look after number one was the fashion there.
OLD MAN: The Prince shouldn't complain, he followed the fashion.
PEER GYNT: I'm standing here with empty pockets –
OLD MAN: Impossible. The Prince is a beggar man?
PEER GYNT: Scraping the barrel. Sold out. And it's your fault.
OLD MAN: Shot down again. Farewell, I'd better work my way
    to town –
PEER GYNT: What will you do?
OLD MAN: I'm going on the stage. There's a demand for the
    ethnic type.
PEER GYNT: Good luck. If I make it through, I might end up
    there. I'll write a farce, mad, profound, and I'll call it
    Gloria Mundi, Her Rise and Fall.

SCENE 9

A crossroads.

BUTTONMOULDER: Now, Peer Gynt, where are the references?
PEER GYNT: Have we arrived at the crossroads? That came
    quickly.
BUTTONMOULDER: I can read your face like a wanted poster.
PEER GYNT: I got tired running about, losing my way.
BUTTONMOULDER: Yes, where does it lead? Well, shall we get
    down to it?
PEER GYNT: One question. What is it to be oneself?
BUTTONMOULDER: Strange coming from your mouth –
PEER GYNT: A short and sweet answer, please.

BUTTONMOULDER: To be oneself is to lose oneself. That's probably wasted on you. So let's just say, shine the Master's light.

PEER GYNT: What about those who never found out what the Master wanted with them?

BUTTONMOULDER: Their instincts should tell them.

PEER GYNT: Instincts often come to nothing. Then you go under half-way through your journey.

BUTTONMOULDER: And there the devil's waiting to hook you up.

PEER GYNT: A complex business. Listen, how can I prove I've been myself? I can't, that's lost. Just now, roaming on the heath, I felt my conscience pinch like a shoe. I said to myself, you are a sinner after all.

BUTTONMOULDER: Are you starting over again?

PEER GYNT: Definitely not. I mean a real sinner, in deed, in thought, in word. I led a dreadful life abroad.

BUTTONMOULDER: Perhaps. May I see the accounts?

PEER GYNT: Let me find a priest and I'll bring you the reckoning.

BUTTONMOULDER: Bring that and you'll be saved from the ladle. But I have orders, Peer –

PEER GYNT: That's from earlier days. Then I led a stupid, lazy life, pretending I was a prophet, believing in fate. Can I try?

BUTTONMOULDER: The next crossroads then, and no further.

PEER GYNT: A priest, even if I've to grab him by the throat. Who'd have thought my sins would save me? It's fire and frying-pan still, but they say where there's life there's hope.

SCENE 10

A hill, covered with heather. The road weaves along the ridge. A thin person with a priest's cassock tucked up and a birdcatcher's net over his shoulder runs along the hill.

THIN MAN: What wouldn't one do to win a soul?

PEER GYNT: Reverend, may I keep you company for a while?

THIN MAN: With pleasure. I enjoy company.

PEER GYNT: I have something on my mind.

THIN MAN: Go on.

PEER GYNT: You see a decent man before you, never did a day inside, but sometimes one loses one's footing – and stumbles.

THIN MAN: That happens to the best, alas.

PEER GYNT: Look, these trifles –

THIN MAN: Trifles?

PEER GYNT: I kept away from outright sin.

THIN MAN: Then my good man, leave me. I am not who you suppose.

PEER GYNT: Were you born with that hoof?

THIN MAN: I flatter myself I was.

PEER GYNT: (*Raises his hat*) I could have sworn you were a priest, and instead I have the honour – well all's for the best.

THIN MAN: Shake hands, a tolerant man. How can I help you? Don't ask for money. I can't provide. You would not believe how slack business is. Complete standstill. No supply of souls. Once in a while the odd one –

PEER GYNT: Has humanity improved itself?

THIN MAN: On the contrary, worse than ever. Most of them end up in the ladle.

PEER GYNT: I have actually heard of this ladle. It's the reason I came –

THIN MAN: Then speak up.

PEER GYNT: I should like –

THIN MAN: A place to stay?

PEER GYNT: You've guessed.

THIN MAN: A warm room?

PEER GYNT: Not too warm. Leave to go, when things look up.

THIN MAN: My dear fellow, I am so sorry, but you would not

believe how many similarly worded petitions people send
me when they are about to shake off the mortal coil.

PEER GYNT: But for my past life I deserve to be let in –

THIN MAN: Trifles.

PEER GYNT: But the slave trade I –

THIN MAN: Some traded in the human mind. They weren't let
in. The ladle, I'm afraid.

PEER GYNT: I left a drowning man to die –

THIN MAN: Now, don't be cross. Your sins were petty.

PEER GYNT: Maybe but –

THIN MAN: It's true, and I have to be on my way. I have to
fetch a nice fat sinner –

PEER GYNT: How has he stuffed himself with sins?

THIN MAN: Night and day he's been himself. That's the
clincher.

PEER GYNT: Dare I ask his name?

THIN MAN: Written here is Peter Gynt.

PEER GYNT: Mr Gynt himself?

THIN MAN: So he swears.

PEER GYNT: Can he be trusted, the same Mr Peter?

THIN MAN: You know him?

PEER GYNT: One knows so many, yes.

THIN MAN: My time's short, where did you see him last?

PEER GYNT: Down at the Cape.

THIN MAN: Capetown? Good Hope?

PEER GYNT: Yes, he's planning to sail from it soon.

THIN MAN: Then I'm away there, I hope I catch him. I hate
Capetown, full of nasty missionaries. (*He rushes off
southwards.*)

PEER GYNT: Stupid bastard. Look at him running with his
tongue hanging out. I put his nose out of joint. He won't
boss me. He'll fall off his high horse. Not that I'm too
secure in the saddle. Kicked out of the class of self-
possessed man. (*He sees a star falling and nods to it.*) Brother
star, greetings from Peer Gynt. We're light, we dim, we die

in darkness. (*He shudders fearfully, walks deeper through the mists in silence and then screams*.) Is there none out there, not one in the whole multitude, not one in the pit, none in heaven? (*He throws his hat on the road and tears his hair. He quietens down by and by.*) Poor soul, go back to nothing, vanish into mist. Earth, full of wonders, forgive that I tramped your grass in vain. Sun, full of wonder, you've wasted your light touching a house whose owner was never at home. Earth, Sun, most beautiful, why did you shine at my mother's birth? Spirit mean and nature wasteful, it is rough to pay for your birth with the price of your life. Let me rise to the highest peak. I want to see the sun rise again. I want to look on the promised land until I am tired. I will see to it that snow drifts over me. They can write above it, no one lives here. And afterwards – afterwards – let life go on its own way.

(*Crossroads.*)

BUTTONMOULDER: Good morning, Peer Gynt. Where is the account of your sins.

PEER GYNT: Everything has run out. The owl smells a rat. Can you hear it hooting? (*Pointing*) What is that shining?

BUTTONMOULDER: A light in a house.

PEER GYNT: What is that sound?

BUTTONMOULDER: A woman singing.

PEER GYNT: There, yes there, is my sin's reckoning.

(*The* BUTTONMOULDER *grabs him.*)

BUTTONMOULDER: Put your house in order.

PEER GYNT: My house, in order, there it is. Go. Were your ladle big as a chest, it still wouldn't have room for me and my doings.

BUTTONMOULDER: The third time the roads cross, Peer. Then –

(PEER GYNT *approaches the house.*)

PEER GYNT: (*Stops*) No. It's wild, it's like a lament, it never stops, go in, go back, go home. Go the round way, the voice said. (*He hears singing from the cabin.*) No, this time straight through, no matter how narrow the road. (*He runs towards the house.*)

(SOLVEIG *comes out of the door, dressed for church, a hymn book in a cloth. With a stick in her hand, she stands straight and still.* PEER GYNT *throws himself down on the threshold.*)

PEER GYNT: If you judge sinners, speak it now.

SOLVEIG: He is here. He is here. Praise be to God. (*She reaches, fumbling, towards him.*)

PEER GYNT: I have offended you. Judge me.

SOLVEIG: My only son, you've not sinned at all.

BUTTONMOULDER: The reckoning, Peer Gynt.

PEER GYNT: Shout out my guilt.

(SOLVEIG *sits down with him.*)

SOLVEIG: You've sung my life so beautifully to me. Blessed be you that's here at last. Blessed, blessed be this Sunday morning. This Whit we meet.

PEER GYNT: Then I am lost.

SOLVEIG: There is one who rules us all.

PEER GYNT: (*Laughs*) Lost, unless you can answer riddles.

SOLVEIG: Ask.

PEER GYNT: Ask? Yes. Can you tell where Peer Gynt has been since last time?

SOLVEIG: Been?

PEER GYNT: Been since he sprang forth from the mind of God, the mark of his maker on his brow? Can you tell me that? If not, I must go home.

SOLVEIG: (*Smiles*) That's an easy riddle.

PEER GYNT: Then say what you know. Where was I, myself alone? With God's mark on my brow, where was I?

SOLVEIG: In my faith, in my hope and in my love.

PEER GYNT: (*Starts back*) What are you saying? Did you mother the child inside me?

SOLVEIG: Yes. But who was his father? It's him who hears when the mother prays, and he forgives.

(*A shaft of light passes over* PEER GYNT.)

PEER GYNT: (*Cries out*) Did you breed me? Did you wife me?
Mother, woman, hide me in your innocence, hide me. (*He
clings to her and hides his face in her lap.*)
(*There is a long silence. The sun rises.*)

SOLVEIG: (*Sings quietly*) My own soft boy, sleep and sleep,
My hand's my eyes to wean and see.

The boy sat on his mother's knee,
The two played through life's long sleep.

The boy drank from his mother's breast,
In life's long sleep, God grant him joy.

The boy did breathe his mother's breath,
Through life's long sleep, my tired boy.

My own soft boy, sleep and sleep
My hand's my eyes to wean and see.
(*The* BUTTONMOULDER'S *voice is heard.*)

BUTTONMOULDER: The final crossroads, Peer, there we'll meet,
and we'll see if – I'll say no more.
(SOLVEIG *sings louder in the light of dawn.*)

SOLVEIG: My hand's my eyes to see and wean,
My own soft boy, sleep and dream.